30-SECOND
PARIS

30-SECOND PARIS

The 50 key elements that
shaped the city, each explained
in half a minute

Editor
John Flower

Foreword
Pierre Boisard

Contributors
Elizabeth Benjamin
Emma Bielecki
Marcelline Block
Sophie Bostock
David Drake
Hugh Dauncey
John Flower
Nicholas Hewitt
Gillian Jein
David Looseley
Luis de Miranda
Nigel Ritchie
Chris Rogers
Niamh Sweeney
Anthony Ward
Nina Wardleworth

Illustrations
Nicky Ackland-Snow

IVY PRESS

First published in the UK in 2018 by
Ivy Press
An imprint of The Quarto Group
The Old Brewery, 6 Blundell Street
London N7 9BH, United Kingdom
T (0)20 7700 6700 F (0)20 7700 8066
www.quartoknows.com

British Library Cataloguing-in-
Publication Data
A catalogue record for this
book is available from the
British Library.

ISBN: 978-1-78240-544-3

This book was conceived,
designed and produced by
Ivy Press
58 West Street, Brighton BN1 2RA, UK

Publisher **Susan Kelly**
Creative Director **Michael Whitehead**
Editorial Director **Tom Kitch**
Art Director **Wayne Blades**
Project Editor **Caroline Earle**
Designer **Ginny Zeal**
Commissioning Editor **Stephanie Evans**
Picture Researcher **Katie Greenwood**
Glossaries **John Flower**
Assistant Editor **Jenny Campbell**

Cover images: Shutterstock/Premier Photo (BG);
/Ints Vikmanis (CL); /Giorgio Morara (FL).

Typeset in Section

Printed in China

10 9 8 7 6 5 4 3 2 1

CONTENTS

FOREWORD

Pierre Boisard

Thirty-five years ago I became a Parisian, fulfilling a dream I had when I was young that would free me from the boredom of life in the country. The only parts of the capital I knew were the Eiffel Tower, the Louvre and the tiny streets of the Quartier Latin. But that was enough for me to succumb to the charm of Paris and to wish desperately to live there. That my tiny attic room was uncomfortable during my first months in the city didn't bother me; I was realizing my dream. I would roam for hours through the streets, unaware of the noise, the dust and the uneven pavements, so taken was I by the magical atmosphere of the places where my steps took me. Today, after many years spent in Paris, the magic has less of a hold; habits and daily routine have finally made their mark. I can pass by those same marvels that once stopped me in my tracks. And yet, in spite of the depressing sight of the Montparnasse tower, I still only have to cross the Pont Neuf or catch a glimpse of the church of Saint-Germain-des-Prés to be consumed by emotion and sense the keen pleasure that had so overwhelmed me when I first saw them.

This powerful charm, which draws millions of tourists to Paris every year, cannot be explained simply by prestigious monuments, venerable churches and a dynamic cultural life. It's quite easy to understand how visitors can be entranced by Notre-Dame or the Louvre or be fascinated by the major museums but how can we explain that they are also drawn to and captivated by those dark alleyways with their decrepit buildings that no guide ever mentions? The only explanation must be some mysterious pull. It is that same pull that six thousand years ago made a handful of men stop on the banks of the Seine and put up a few temporary huts. They could have settled further up or down the river but they stopped at this precise spot, which was still uninhabited. A charm made them stay, just as it has their descendants and all those who have ventured onto these banks.

In spite of invasions, fires, riots and epidemics, a human presence has been constant, the town has grown, it has been the seat of royalty and magnificent monuments have been built. That could not have happened elsewhere in France. Each period has made its mark: Philippe-Auguste's Louvre, the Tour Saint-Jacques, the Sainte-Chapelle, Baron Haussmann's boulevards, the Tuileries and even the indigestible meringue that is the Sacré-Cœur overlooking Montmartre. And equally characteristic are those seedy side streets with their inns so popular with the light-hearted student friends of the medieval poet François Villon. Paris is simply that: a magical place where you can sense the presence of all those who have lived there over the centuries. It is that which gives today's Parisians an intense desire to live as fully as possible, to crowd onto café terraces, sports grounds and entertainment venues in spite of the bloody attacks that have thrown the city into mourning.

I'm no longer surprised at the crowds of tourists who queue to visit the catacombs in order to gaze at the piles of human bones and skulls. It is not because of some morbid taste that they throng there but because they sense that these thousands of unknown dead who bear witness to the capital's past life with its turbulence and its many mysteries have not deserted their ancient dwellings. To visit Paris is not just a matter of admiring its churches, palaces and monuments, nor of strolling about the streets or wandering along the banks of the Seine, it is to allow yourself to be overcome by the mysterious charm of these places and to be aware of the sounds from bygone centuries.

Parisian charm
A panorama of Paris from the Parc Montsouris – a city that has delighted and inspired over the centuries.

INTRODUCTION
John Flower

Paris can claim to be the most visited of Europe's capital cities, rivalled only perhaps by London. Popularly known as the City of Light or the City of Love, Paris's beauty, charm, intellectual and artistic life and even its mysteries have long fascinated and seduced. Four hundred years ago, the French philosopher Michel de Montaigne described Paris as one of the 'noblest ornaments of the world'; in the nineteenth century, it was noted by novelists Honoré de Balzac for its elegance and Charles Dickens for being 'extraordinary'. More recently, for Henry Miller, it was a 'paradise'; Scott Fitzgerald marvelled at its 'intelligence and good manners'; and Ernest Hemingway found inspiration here for his collection of memoirs, *A Moveable Feast*. Nor has Paris been neglected by the cinema, as is witnessed by such iconic productions as Marcel Carné's *Les Enfants du paradis* (1945), Jean-Luc Godard's *À bout de souffle* (*Breathless*, 1960) and, in this century, by Jean-Pierre Jeunet's *Le Fabuleux Destin d'Amélie Poulain* (*Amélie*, 2001) and Woody Allen's *Midnight in Paris* (2011).

Such credentials speak for themselves, but if there were any doubt about Paris's continuing appeal for the millions of tourists who flock here each year, a glance at the shelves of the city's many bookstores would soon dispel it. There are countless serious academic studies, glossy popular historical surveys, collections of photographs, of posters or of the memoirs of the good and the great who have lived and worked here. Not unreasonably, therefore, we can ask whether another book is either necessary or even useful. This book answers that question affirmatively.

Written by specialists, its seven chapters are informative and up to date, frequently highlighting events and details that are elsewhere neglected or ignored. The first chapter, **History**, creates a historical frame for the city from its origins through some of the significant social and political events that have shaped it – such as the 1789 Revolution and the Occupation by the Nazis (1940–4) – to the present day and gives a glimpse of the future. Chapter two, **Quartiers**, offers an overview of its cosmopolitan *quartiers*, and the third chapter, **The Seine & Open Spaces**,

Parisian pleasure

Paris has always been a magnet for intellectuals, artists and pleasure seekers. The hilltop district of Montmartre, with its music halls and cabarets, together with the Sacré-Cœur basilica, is the epitome of belle-époque Paris.

on the Seine, with its banks, bridges and islands, and the city's open spaces, gives a sense of Paris's reflective side, where books are bought and people take exercise or wander simply for pleasure. In chapter four, **Markets**, are broad-brush descriptions of the different kinds of markets, from flea markets to decidedly upmarket department stores. Together, these chapters provide the context into which outstanding examples of art and architecture and of various forms of entertainment can be placed (**Art & Architecture** and **Museums & Entertainment**). The final chapter, **Around Paris**, takes us beyond the city's walls and includes entries on the famous royal château of Versailles and the popular attractions of Euro-Disney and the Parc d'Astérix and as well as St-Denis' Stade de France and the clay courts of Roland-Garros, two unmissable venues for followers of the sporting calendar. Each chapter is prefaced by a glossary of technical or unfamiliar words and phrases and contains a profile of an eminent or influential figure from history, art, literature or the entertainment world who has left their stamp on the city as we know it.

How to use this book

Each of the 50 sharply focused topics is intended to be read in just half a minute – the time it takes to read 300 words – and each adopts the same, easily assimilated approach: a single sentence, the 3-Second Perspective, succinctly summarizing the topic; a pithy main paragraph, the 30-Second City, providing the detail; with a shorter one, the 3-Minute Sojourn, providing a wider context and inviting further investigation. Mini biographies of key eminent or influential individuals complete the picture. Facing-page illustrations from a variety of sources reflect the content of each topic. Readers are, of course, at liberty to start at the beginning or simply to open the book at random and follow their noses, as it were – exactly like a walk through the city itself.

If ever a reason were needed for visiting Paris, it would be to satisfy the appetite for urban life with all its riches. As Hemingway observed, Paris is a moveable feast for the senses, offering fashion stores and food halls, architecture and art, exhibitions and entertainment, palaces and parks, by way of busy boulevards, quiet gardens and cemeteries. *Bonne visite*!

Artistic spirit

Paris has inspired artists for centuries, and the city is home to many of the world's masterpieces of art and architecture. The Musée d'Orsay is a must-see attraction for its architecture as well as for its art collection.

HISTORY

HISTORY
GLOSSARY

banlieue The suburbs of more prosperous urban centres, often originally the sites of industrial development. While some have slowly become gentrified, others remain deprived and are areas of social and political unrest. *Banlieue rouge* (red) denotes suburbs that have left-wing, often communist, sympathies.

Commune A radical, revolutionary, largely working-class uprising that formed a government in Paris between 18 March and 28 May 1871 during the siege of the capital by the Prussian army and in the wake of the defeat of France and the collapse of the Second Empire in 1870. It was supported by the National Guard, which refused an armistice and was violently suppressed by the Army in May 1871 in a week known as 'la semaine sanglante'.

Estates-General (*États-généraux*) A general assembly with three bodies: the clergy, the aristocracy and the common people (the peasantry and the bourgeoisie). Unused since the seventeenth century, the assembly was recalled in 1789 by Louis XVI but was quickly deemed undemocratic with the result that with the result that all three bodies were amalgamated as the National Assembly.

Free French (*France libre*) The movement formed by Charles de Gaulle in June 1940 after he had refused to accept the terms of Philippe Pétain's armistice and had fled to London. Here he also formed the *Forces françaises libres*, whose members joined the Resistance and played a decisive role in the liberation of Paris in 1944.

Grand Paris Express Although linked to President Mitterrand's *grands projets* (see page 30), the *Grand Paris Express* is a plan to improve the quality of life for the 8.5 million people daily working in the capital by 2030. In addition to massive expansion of the Métro system, areas of cultural activity are planned.

League of Patriots (*Ligue des Patriotes*) A nationalist movement founded in 1882 as a reaction to France's defeat in the Franco-Prussian war. At times xenophobic and anti-Semitic, it experienced moments of crisis and had fluctuating support before it was disbanded in 1939.

Maillotins Workers and peasants who, in 1382, rose in armed protest against an increase in taxes under Charles VI. The revolt, which began in Paris, was violent but lasted for less than a year. The name derives from *maillet*, a club used in combat, but was not applied until the sixteenth century.

Préfecture de Police An independent body established in Paris in 1800 that answers to the Ministry of the Interior but has responsibility for the overall security of the capital and surrounding *départements*.

rafles Mass arrests. The most notorious during the Occupation was of 13,000 Jews carried out by French police on 16–17 July 1942. Those arrested were packed into the *vélodrome d'hiver* (cycle stadium) before being sent to Drancy or concentration camps.

rapprochement In addition to the political allegiances of the Popular Front (1936–8), Maurice Thorez, the leader of the Communist Party, appealed to Catholics, encouraging them to join him to work for a more equal society.

Second Empire (1852–70) The period under Louis-Napoléon (Napoléon III) that saw a return to a monarchical constitution and a period of colonial expansion. The last ten years were more liberal, Baron Haussmann was appointed to oversee the reconstruction of Paris and commercial enterprises flourished, notably in the creation of departmental stores. With the defeat of France, Napoléon was briefly imprisoned in Germany before being exiled in England, where he died in 1873.

The Terror The period September 1793–July 1794 when tens of thousands considered to be opposed to the Revolution and enemies of the Republic were guillotined. It was viewed as a vital instrument of the revolutionary government.

Third Estate A term in existence since 1302 adopted by Abbé Emmanuel Sieyès for a pamphlet (*Qu'est-ce que le tiers état?*) published in January 1789 in response to proposed tax reforms. It argues that of the three bodies in the Estates-General, the third, with elected members from more than 90 per cent of the population, was the best to represent the nation.

Tuileries A royal and imperial palace, the first parts of which were built in the sixteenth century. Much enlarged, it saw the declaration of the First Republic (1792–1804) but was largely destroyed by fire during the Commune in 1871. Various proposals for it to be rebuilt have come to nothing.

Third Republic (1870–1940) A system of government originally intended to be provisional but that became the longest, ending only with the defeat and occupation of France by the Germans in 1940. Subject to crises, scandals and political extremes on both the left and the right, it has been widely regarded by historians as weak and decadent.

GALLO-ROMAN PARIS

the 30-second city

Caesar's Gallic War commentary
for 53 and 52 BCE mentioned Lutetia, a settlement
of the Parisii tribe located on an island in the
Seine, whose inhabitants burnt the town and
bridges in anticipation of Roman attack.
Traditionally, Lutetia is equated with Île de la
Cité, although the suburb of Nanterre emerges
as a contender following recent archaeological
discoveries. Post-conquest construction of a
Roman-style town with regular street grids
began on rising ground beyond the Left Bank
opposite Île de la Cité. Vestiges of the Thermes
de Cluny (public baths) and the Arènes de Lutèce
(an amphitheatre) remain as testimony to
monumental architecture, which also included an
aqueduct, a forum and temples, with necropoli
beyond the town. Decorative motifs of river
barges at the Cluny baths indicate the importance
of riverine trade, complemented by a practical
crossing of the Seine. In the mid-third century CE,
Christianity arrived and, during Imperial
persecution of Christians, Bishop Denis was
martyred, reputedly on a hill that became
Martyrs Mount – Montmartre. Late in the third
century CE, Gaul began to experience Germanic
tribal incursions. The readily defended Île de la
Cité was favoured with walls and became the
settlement focus at the expense of the vulnerable
Left Bank. Conserved excavated remains of the
period are publicly accessible beneath the Parvis
– the paved area in front of Notre-Dame.

RELATED TOPICS
See also
MONTMARTRE
page 38

ISLANDS
page 54

SAINT-DENIS
page 142

3-SECOND BIOGRAPHIES
SAINT DENIS
d. c. 250 CE
First bishop of Paris, the
decapitated martyr fabulously
walked away from the place of
execution clutching his head and
preaching, becoming the focus
of a widespread medieval cult

CLOVIS
d. c. 511 CE
King of the Franks and founder
of the Merovingian dynasty,
with sway over large parts
of previously Roman Gaul.
After his death, power was
dissipated between his sons

30-SECOND TEXT
Anthony Ward

*Early accounts describe
the settlement of
Lutetia in Roman Gaul,
which was later
renamed Paris.*

3-SECOND PERSPECTIVE
An outline narrative of
the early settlement that
becomes Paris can be
sketched using an amalgam
of sources – ancient texts,
traditional histories and
archaeology.

3-MINUTE SOJOURN
Early in the fourth century
CE, Lutetia was known as
City of the Parisii, a pretty
unremarkable town within
Roman Gaul, with only
regional significance, its
legacy contributing little
directly to the city's later
national pre-eminence.
Wider political importance
began to be achieved
following the Western
Roman Empire's collapse,
when the Frankish king
Clovis ruled extensive
conquered territory from
Paris for a short period
after c. 500 CE. Arguably,
it was not until the late
900s CE that Paris emerged
as capital of an entity that
can be described as France.

MEDIEVAL PARIS

the 30-second city

3-SECOND PERSPECTIVE
By 1300, Paris had become the glittering, preeminent city in France and Europe, only to decline temporarily due to English invasion, civil war and plague.

3-MINUTE SOJOURN
Medieval Paris owed much of its prosperity to the powerful boat owners, known as *marchands de l'eau*, who supplied the city with products from France and abroad and enjoyed a privileged, if periodically fractious, relationship with the monarchy. With docks along the Right Bank, especially the Place de Grève, and cargo ferries across the river, they became the most powerful of the city's guilds, and their emblem, a ship on a river, surmounted by the royal fleur-de-lys, became the city's coat of arms.

Medieval Paris, in the Île-de-France, established itself as the capital of France and largest city in Europe, with over 200,000 inhabitants in 1328, protected by the walls of Philippe-Auguste (1220) and Charles V (1371). Notre-Dame cathedral (1163–1345), built, like the Sainte-Chapelle (1248), in the new Gothic style, enhanced the city's reputation as an ecclesiastical hub, while the Left Bank housed the internationally famous University of Paris. The Right Bank, with its port, skilled craftsmen, financiers and Les Halles (food market), became a powerful commercial centre, leading French kings to make Paris their capital. Their new fortified palaces extending along the Seine, from the Louvre to the Bastille and Vincennes, were surrounded by the residences of nobles and bishops and, until 1307, the Knights Templar, the King's treasurers. Conflict between the state and the influential merchants culminated in the failed rebellion of Étienne Marcel in 1358, but resurfaced in the anti-taxation *Maillotins* revolt of 1382. The city was also weakened by plague in 1348, rivalry between the Burgundian and Orleanist (Armagnac) factions (1404–36) and the Hundred Years' War (1337–1453), which reduced the population by half by 1422 and induced the court to retrench to the Loire, from where it did not return until 1528.

RELATED TOPICS
See also
LATIN QUARTER
page 46

ISLANDS
page 54

NOTRE-DAME DE PARIS
page 100

3-SECOND BIOGRAPHIES
PHILIPPE-AUGUSTE
1165–1223
King of France (1180–1223), who developed the power of the nation, while consolidating Paris as the capital

ÉTIENNE MARCEL
d. 1358
A wealthy bourgeois, who became Prévot (the equivalent of Lord Mayor) of the Paris merchants in 1354 and, as head of the merchants, worked towards diminishing royal power and fiscal control

30-SECOND TEXT
Nicholas Hewitt

Under the rule of King Philippe-Auguste, Paris was established as the capital of France.

REVOLUTION & TERROR

the 30-second city

Originating out of the King's need to raise more taxes, the first phase of the Revolution involved the recall, in May 1789, of the Estates-General (representing the three Orders of the Church, nobility and Third Estate) to approve these measures. Instead, the Third Estate took control, established the National Assembly, transferring sovereignty from king to nation, and drafted a constitution underpinning key political and legal rights. The second phase saw popular involvement in two key events: the storming of the Bastille prison and the forcible relocation of the royal family from Versailles to Paris. Both actions were the result of volatile crowds and defecting soldiers seeking to take defensive measures against counter-revolution and secure food against a backdrop of scarcity. The third phase was provoked by the king's declining popularity following a failed attempt to flee France in June 1791, which resulted in the storming of the Tuileries in August 1792, his execution and the declaration of a republic. The fourth phase was marked by the creation of a new governing power, known as the Committee of Public Safety, which oversaw 'the Terror', a by-product of political tensions caused by external and internal war. The final phase, marked by Napoléon Bonaparte's *coup d'état* in November 1799, oversaw the transformation of France into an imperial-military state.

RELATED TOPIC
See also
VERSAILLES
page 138

3-SECOND BIOGRAPHIES
EMMANUEL JOSEPH SIEYES
1748–1836
Political theorist and clergyman who played a key role in giving the Third Estate its identity and helping to draft France's new constitution

LOUIS XVI
1754–93
Last king of France (1774–92), whose support for the American War of Independence (1775–83) helped to tip France into bankruptcy and subsequent upheaval

MAXIMILIEN DE ROBESPIERRE
1758–94
Lawyer elected to the Estates-General in 1789 who dominated the powerful Committee for Public Safety, responsible for the Terror, until his downfall

30-SECOND TEXT
Nigel Ritchie

Turbulent times – from 1789 to 1799 Paris saw revolution, the Terror, and a coup d'état.

20 May 1799
Born in Tours

1813
Asked to leave his school, the Collège de Vendôme, owing to an episode of a mysterious psychosomatic illness ascribed variously to excessive reading or excessive masturbation

1814
Moves to Paris with his family and is tutored privately

1816
Enters the Sorbonne

1819
Finishes his legal studies; refuses to become a lawyer

1822
Publishes his first novels under the name Horace de Saint-Aubin

1826
Buys a printworks he imagines will make him rich; its failure will leave him significantly in debt

1829
Publishes *Les Chouans* (*The Chouans*)

1832
Conceives the idea for his magnum opus, originally called *Etudes des mœurs* (*Studies of Manners*), eventually known as *La Comédie humaine* (*The Human Comedy*). Begins correspondence with Ewelina Hanska, a Polish aristocrat

1833
Publishes *Eugénie Grandet* to great critical acclaim

1835
Publishes *Le Père Goriot* (*Old Goriot*)

1836
La Vieille fille (*The Old Maid*) appears in a series of instalments in the newspaper *La Presse*, the first serialized novel in France

1838
Instrumental in setting up the Société des Gens de Lettres, the body formed to protect the rights of authors against greedy publishers and unscrupulous newspaper proprietors

1842
Publishes a preface to *La Comédie humaine*, explaining his ambition of producing a panorama of post-Revolutionary society and detailing the structure of the project

1843
Publishes *Illusions perdues* (*Lost Illusions*)

1848
Leaves Paris for Ukraine; once there his health declines precipitously

1850
Marries his long-time lover Ewelina Hanska; they return to Paris

18 August 1850
Dies in Paris, attended by his mother, his wife and Victor Hugo

HONORÉ DE BALZAC

Born the year Bonaparte seized power, Balzac came to be thought of – not least by himself – as the Napoléon of letters, a man of colossal ambition and energy. Originally from Tours, he came to Paris at the age of 15 when his family settled there, and he remained there for most of the rest of his life (although he did travel in Italy, where he became tangled up in a scheme to reopen abandoned mines, one of his many get-rich plans to end in dismal failure, and in Ukraine, where his lover Mme Ewelina Hanska had an estate).

Balzac studied as a lawyer before making his literary debut pseudonymously as Horace de Saint-Aubin, a sort of second-rate Gallic Walter Scott, and then cut his teeth on Parisian journalism, a world he would later depict in a novel whose title, *Illusions perdues* (*Lost Illusions*), is an eloquent summary of his experiences therein. In 1829, he published *Les Chouans* (*The Chouans*), a story of Royalist guerrillas during the Revolution. This was the first stone in what would come to be the mighty edifice of *La Comédie humaine* (*The Human Comedy*). Balzac conceived of this project, comprising 91 interlocking stories, linked through recurring characters, as a kind of natural history of post-Revolutionary France, describing the behaviour of various social species in their natural habitat. Sometimes that habitat was the provinces, more often it was Paris, imagined not as the City of Light but as the city of appetite, where the frenzied pursuit of pleasure and money, Balzac's chief themes, generated countless narratives. In his depiction of a society in which all traditional ties had been dissolved and the cash nexus was sovereign, Balzac anticipated Marx; in repurposing the novel as a form of proto-sociological enquiry, he pioneered realism.

If *La Comédie humaine* holds a mirror up to the society in which it was produced, then it is a fairground mirror. Balzac's books are peopled by monsters and monomaniacs, distorted, distended, larger-than-life figures in whom are the quintessential tensions and energies of a society still suffering the aftershocks of the Revolution. But he was his own most memorable creation: dressed as a monk, drinking endless cups of coffee to fuel 12-, 15- and 19-hour working days, Balzac became a legend, half-Stakhanov, toiling to produce the serialized novels the public demanded, half-demiurge. He died, exhausted, in 1850 and is buried in Père Lachaise cemetery, overlooking Paris.

Emma Bielecki

THE BELLE ÉPOQUE

the 30-second city

RELATED TOPICS
See also
MONTMARTRE
page 38

HENRI DE TOULOUSE-
LAUTREC
page 86

GRAND PALAIS & PETIT PALAIS
page 122

3-SECOND BIOGRAPHIES
PAUL DÉROULÈDE
1846–1914
Nationalist leader of the
League of Patriots

ALFRED DREYFUS
1859–1935
Jewish army officer tried and
wrongly convicted (in 1894)
of treason but pardoned in
1906

JEAN JAURÈS
1859–1914
Left-wing politician, leader
of the French Socialist Party,
orator and anti-war campaigner
assassinated in 1914

3-SECOND PERSPECTIVE
With its top hats and
crinolines, frivolity
and modernity, the
period 1870–1914 was
nostalgically remembered,
despite economic and
political turbulence, as
a lost golden age.

3-MINUTE SOJOURN
After Haussmann's
urbanization projects
of the Second Empire, the
demographic composition
of Belle-Époque Paris
changed even more, with
the acceleration of the
movement of artisans and
workers out of the centre
to outlying districts like
Belleville or Ménilmontant,
or beyond the city to the
industrial suburbs or
banlieue rouge. They were
replaced by a growing
bourgeoisie and a new
white-collar class who
became one of the main
consumers of the new
forms of mass-cultural
activity.

After the Prussian siege (1870)
and the Commune (1871), Paris entered an
apparently glittering period, lasting until the
outbreak of war in 1914. As the capital of the
new Third Republic, it dominated the national
and international stage, especially through
the exhibitions of 1889 and 1900, which
showcased France's technological and artistic
supremacy, with lasting icons like the Eiffel
Tower and the Grand Palais. Electricity powered
the new Métro system, revolutionized street
lighting and created the 'Ville Lumière' – a
tourist and entertainment capital captured by
Toulouse-Lautrec and visited by aristocrats
and millionaires from France and overseas.
The Sacré-Cœur dominated the skyline, while
exclusive apartments, luxury fashion houses,
hotels and restaurants centred on the Champs-
Élysées embodied Parisian chic. Culturally,
Paris dominated the visual arts, from Post-
Impressionism to Cubism, accompanied by
flowerings in music, literature, theatre and the
newly invented cinema. Underneath, however,
were severe cracks: sluggish economic growth
and financial instability, the anti-Semitism of
the Dreyfus Affair (1894), the Panama Canal
scandal (1892), the rise of extremism on the
Right (with Boulanger, Déroulède and Maurras)
and challenges on the left from Jaurès's socialist
party, labour unrest and anarchist activity.

30-SECOND TEXT
Nicholas Hewitt

*Technical and artistic
innovation epitomized
the golden age of the
Belle Époque in Paris.*

BETWEEN THE WARS

the 30-second city

3-SECOND PERSPECTIVE
Mounting social and
political unrest between
the ending of one war
against Germany and the
start of another coincided
with an avant-garde
cultural explosion.

3-MINUTE SOJOURN
Paris's unsurpassed
reputation for artistic and
sexual freedom acted like
a magnet to cutting-edge
national and international
writers and artists.
New movements were
spawned or developed–
Cubism (Picasso, Braque),
Surrealism (Dali, Breton,
Duchamp, Man Ray),
Art Deco and Modern
Architecture (Le Corbusier).
While penning *Ulysses*,
Irish novelist James Joyce
mixed with American
ex-pats F. Scott Fitzgerald,
Gertrude Stein, Ezra Pound,
Ford Madox Ford and
Ernest Hemingway, whose
memoir, *A Moveable Feast*,
captured these heady days.

After the war, Paris expanded,
following the demolition of its old fortified walls
and the growth of its industrial suburbs. The low
post-war birth rate held the city's population at
below three million, despite the influx of thousands
of immigrants from Russia, central and southern
Europe – especially Italy. A ten-year economic
boom from 1921 ushered in the *années folles*
(the Crazy Years), epitomized by glamorous
music-hall star Josephine Baker. This coincided
with the re-establishment of Paris as the world's
cultural capital, whose epicentre shifted from
Montmartre to Montparnasse. The city's global
importance was reinforced by its staging of the
Olympic Games (1924) and three international
exhibitions (1925, 1931 and 1937). The Great
Depression hit France from 1931, bringing
mounting political and economic tensions.
The scandal-ridden parliamentary regime of the
Third Republic came under attack from the left
– the French Communist Party, founded in 1920 –
and from far-right anti-Semitic leagues, who
attempted to storm the parliament on 6 February
1934. Rapprochement between French Communists
and Socialists led to the creation of the Popular
Front (1936–8), which introduced significant
social reforms – paid holidays and shorter
working hours – before collapsing in a country
and continent increasingly polarized between
Communism and Fascism.

RELATED TOPICS
See also
MONTPARNASSE
page 36

MONTMARTRE
page 38

3-SECOND BIOGRAPHIES
JAMES JOYCE
1842–1941
Irish writer whose novel
Ulysses (1922) was published in
Paris by Sylvia Beach from her
bookshop Shakespeare and
Company in the Rue de l'Odéon

PABLO PICASSO
1871–1973
Spanish painter and sculptor.
One of the most influential
artists of the twentieth century

ANDRÉ BRETON
1896–1966
French poet and art critic.
Founder and chief theorist of
Surrealism and author of *The
Surrealist Manifesto* (1924)

30-SECOND TEXT
David Drake

*Creatives, including
dancer Josephine Baker,
were among the ex-pat
Americans who settled in
Paris during the Crazy Years.*

OCCUPATION & LIBERATION

the 30-second city

On 14 June 1940, the German army (*Wehrmacht*) occupied Paris. Parisians were subject to German directives and laws passed by Marshal Pétain's pro-collaboration government based in Vichy. Initially, most Parisians adopted a wait-and-see attitude, but a few minuscule resistance groups began publishing clandestine newspapers and helping Allied servicemen to escape from France. As Occupation progressed, most Parisians suffered increasing deprivations – notably of food, clothing and fuel – while access to a steady supply of black market luxury goods allowed a wealthy minority to maintain its extravagant lifestyle. Following the German invasion of Russia (June 1941), the French Communist Party initiated a policy of assassinating German soldiers, to which the German army responded with savage reprisals. Repressive measures against Jews also escalated with mass arrests (*rafles*) carried out by the Paris police. From exile in London, General Charles de Gaulle, who refused to accept the armistice or recognize the Vichy government, urged patience but failed to prevent the launching of a Paris anti-German insurrection on 19 August 1944. On 25 August, Free French tanks and American troops entered the city, de Gaulle arrived and the Germans surrendered. The following day, acclaimed by massive crowds, de Gaulle led a triumphal march down the Champs-Élysées.

3-SECOND PERSPECTIVE
The German occupation of Paris lasted from 14 June 1940 until 25 August 1944, when the Paris Resistance, Free French forces and the Allies liberated the city.

3-MINUTE SOJOURN
Today, reminders of the Occupation and Liberation proliferate: wall plaques recall those Parisians killed during the Liberation, shell damage to the walls of the Préfecture de Police (Police headquarters) and other buildings remains clearly visible, statues commemorate the Resistance and streets are named after individual resisters and Resistance groups. Over half the 11,400 Jewish children deported from France and killed in Auschwitz were Parisians: plaques near school entrances now recognize the Vichy government's responsibility in this crime.

RELATED TOPIC
See also
DRANCY
page 148

3-SECOND BIOGRAPHIES
MARSHAL PHILIPPE PÉTAIN
1856–1951
First World War hero. Head of Vichy government committed to collaboration with Germany. Sentenced to death for treason in August 1945. Sentence commuted by de Gaulle to life-imprisonment

GENERAL CHARLES DE GAULLE
1890–1970
Leader of Free French in London and Algiers (1940–4). Head of Provisional French government (1944–6). Founded the Fifth French Republic (1958) and was its president until he resigned in 1969

30-SECOND TEXT
David Drake

During the Occupation, Paris effectively became the German capital of France until the city was liberated in 1944.

DEUTSCHLAND SIEGT AN ALLEN FRONTEN

MODERN PERIOD

the 30-second city

During the '30 glorious years' after the Second World War, President Charles de Gaulle rid Paris of her shantytowns and dilapidated housing, creating high-rise housing projects – the *grands ensembles* – in the suburbs. President François Mitterrand's *grands projets* reshaped the monumental landscape of the city, restoring the Louvre, converting the Gare d'Orsay to a museum and building the Bibliothèque Nationale de France, Institut du Monde Arabe and the business district at La Défense. Since 2007, the *Grand Paris Express* has sought to address the need for transport infrastructures linking centre and suburbs, promising over 200 kilometres (125 miles) of new Métro line by 2030. With decolonization and the end of the Algerian War (1954–62), sustained migration from France's ex-colonies made Paris the most multicultural city in Europe but also occasioned appalling failures of urban government. In October 1961, a peaceful march by the FLN (National Liberation Front) was repressed by the police and resulted in the deaths of at least 200 Algerians. Deindustrialization in the 1970s and 80s led to crisis in the multi-ethnic, working-class suburbs, which today have become emblematic of unemployment, unrest and racial apartheid. As the suburban riots of November 2005 and 2007 and *Charlie Hebdo* and Bataclan attacks of 2015 demonstrate, cultural integration is the most pressing challenge facing Paris today.

3-SECOND PERSPECTIVE
The twin forces of modernization and decolonization have been the most significant in shaping the architectural and cultural topographies of contemporary Paris.

3-MINUTE SOJOURN
Today, flashes of architectural eccentricity punctuate the limestone logic of old Paris. In 1973, the Tour de Montparnasse defied the city's 31-metre (100-foot) height restriction, piercing the urban skyline at 210 metres (690 feet). The 'inside-out' architecture of Renzo Piano's and Richard Rogers' Centre Pompidou (1977) and the glassy contrasts of I. M. Pei's Louvre pyramid (1989) vehemently divided public opinion, but they nevertheless remain among the capital's most visited tourist sites.

RELATED TOPICS
See also
MONTPARNASSE
page 36

BIBLIOTHÈQUE NATIONALE DE FRANCE (BNF)
page 108

MUSÉE DU LOUVRE
page 124

MUSÉE D'ORSAY
page 132

LA DÉFENSE
page 140

3-SECOND BIOGRAPHY
FRANÇOIS MITTERRAND
1916–96
Leader of the Socialist Party and France's longest-serving president (1981–95). Nicknamed 'Mitteramses I' by the satirical newspaper *Le Canard enchaîné* during the construction of the Louvre pyramid

30-SECOND TEXT
Gillian Jein

The cultural and social modernization of Paris has thrown up many challenges.

JE SUIS CHARLIE

MAHOMET
CHARLIE
PARDONNE À...

QUARTIERS

14 July 1789 Commonly held to be the day when the Revolution was triggered, this was the day when the Bastille, formerly a fourteenth-century fortress, subsequently a prison and a symbol of oppression, was attacked by an angry mob pushed to insurrection. Demolished within a year, the Bastille would remain a central feature of all subsequent historical and fictional accounts of the Revolution. July 14 remains France's major national holiday.

arrondissement An administrative district with its own council and elected mayor. An initial 12 were created in Paris in 1795 and increased to 20 in 1759 under Napoléon III. They differ in size and population, and in 2016, the mayor, Anne Hildago, proposed a conflation of the first four into a single administrative unit by 2020, though each would retain its number. Lyon and Marseille are the only two other French towns to have numbered *arrondissements*.

Art Nouveau A style of art and architecture developed in the late nineteenth and early twentieth centuries in reaction to earlier traditional forms. Characterized by the use of colour and flowing forms, it is often inspired by the natural world. The entrances to Guimard's Métro stations are an example.

bobo A contraction of *bourgeois* and *bohème* (bohemian bourgeois) and a slightly pejorative term to describe a particular lifestyle.

catacombs The vast area of tunnels, former quarries of limestone excavated since the Middle Ages as Paris expanded. From the late eighteenth century, a section in the 14th *arrondissement* was turned into an ossuary as graveyards elsewhere in Paris became a health hazard. A section nearly two kilometres (a mile) long, and now a museum beneath the Place Denfert-Rochereau, is carefully arranged with corridors and open spaces. Although officially closed, the rest of the network (around 300 kilometres/180 miles) is illegally used for various activities by those known as *cataphiles*.

Commune A radical revolutionary and largely working-class uprising that formed a government in Paris between 18 March and 28 May 1871 during the siege of the capital by the Prussian army and in the wake of the defeat of France and the collapse of the Second Empire in 1870. It was supported by the National Guard which refused an armistice and was violently suppressed by the Army in May 1871 in a week known as '*la semaine sanglante*'.

Customs Wall The Mur des Fermiers Généraux was built between 1784 and 1791 to enforce import duty on goods, and especially on alcohol, being brought into the city. It was eventually destroyed during Haussmann's urban developments, but traces of the original 62 toll barriers remain in the Parc Monceau (8th *arrondissement*) and the Place Denfert-Rochereau (14th).

fin de siècle While this phrase literally means the end of any century, it is normally used to include the first years of the following. In France, it traditionally applies to the end of the nineteenth and beginning of the twentieth centuries, a period generally considered to be characterized by unrest and decadence.

gare French for train station. Paris has six major railway stations serving the provinces and abroad. The Métro and RER (Réseau Express Régional, the rapid transit system linking city centre and suburbs) line stations are known as *stations*.

grandes écoles Unlike universities, entry to these schools, which are sometimes referred to as 'superior', is by competitive examination. They were created in the eighteenth century to provide training for key ministerial posts, a function that is continued to the point that, while their quality is widely recognized, they have been criticized for their endogamous practice.

guinguettes Cheap establishments for eating, drinking and entertainment, often by a river, originally outside the capital's walls and therefore not subject to taxes. They developed in the eighteenth century and became particularly popular in the late nineteenth and early twentieth centuries.

'Haussmannization' Reference to Haussmann's programme of renovation of Paris for the betterment of society.

hôtel In addition to its normal English meaning, the word can describe a detached private mansion (*hôtel particulier*) and also administrative buildings such as Hôtel de Ville (town hall) or Hôtel des Impôts (tax office).

Parc de Buttes-Chaumont The hugely popular park in the 19th *arrondissement* that was constructed in the 1860s on the site of a former refuse/sewage tip and quarries as part of Haussmann's urban developments. Landscaped by Jean-Charles Alphand, its features include a lake with an island (accessible by bridges), grottos, waterfalls, steep hills and cliffs. On the island is the Temple de Sibylle, a copy of the Vesta Temple in Tivoli, Italy. The park is cut by part of the tracks of the now-defunct Chemin de fer de Petite Ceinture – the railway line that once circled the city.

MONTPARNASSE

the 30-second city

Nicknamed by students in the mid-nineteenth century after the mountain home of the muses in Greek mythology, Montparnasse became, less than a century later, the capital's most cosmopolitan and culturally rich *quartier*, principally covering the 14th *arrondissement* but encroaching into the 5th, 6th, 7th and 15th. By the 1920s, artists and writers, especially from America and Russia, had established ghettos and studios here, traces of which remain. Café life developed apace and continues to be a feature of much social and political activity. Tourists flock to the catacombs, a small part of the medieval quarries adapted from the late eighteenth century to clear older cemeteries. Its parks – Montsouris and Brassens – provide a popular escape for local residents, and the 56th floor of the monolithic Tour Montparnasse affords magnificent views across the city. Like Père Lachaise, Montparnasse's landscaped cemetery, containing the sole survivor of the former numerous windmills in the area, houses the tombs of many artists, writers and politicians. The Rue de la Gaîté has the highest concentration of theatres of any street in Paris while the Porte de Vanves provides the site for a busy flea market at weekends. Continuing a centuries-old tradition, the Gare de Montparnasse maintains easy contact with the southwest and Brittany.

Culturally and politically alive, parts of Montparnasse still retain much of their village atmosphere.

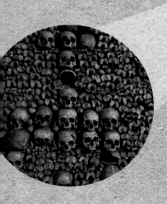

Jean Paul SART
1905 - 1980
—
one DE BEAUV
1908 - 1986

MONTMARTRE

the 30-second city

Once a village and shrine,
Montmartre became prominent after the
construction, in 1784, of the Customs Wall, which
provided cheap alcohol and entertainment along
its periphery. After the extension of Paris in
1860, lower Montmartre's boulevards became
entertainment centres, while upper Montmartre
(the Butte) remained provincial, favoured by
artists, writers, criminals and anarchists.
Rodolphe Salis's cabaret, Le Chat Noir, of 1881,
drew in visitors from Paris and beyond, and
belle-époque Montmartre, with the construction
of the Sacré-Cœur, was also synonymous with
Parisian pleasure, boosted by music-halls like the
Moulin-Rouge, opened in 1889 and attracting
French bourgeois, Americans, Russian and
British aristocrats, and painters, from Renoir
to Toulouse-Lautrec. In the 1900s, the artists
and writers retreated further up the Butte and
congregated in cafés on the Place du Tertre and in
the cabaret Le Lapin Agile, on the Rue des Saules.
After the First World War, while many artists
migrated to Montparnasse, Montmartre remained
popular through American jazz clubs and music-
hall stars like Mistinguett, Maurice Chevalier and
Josephine Baker. By the end of the Second World
War, however, Montmartre had lost its cutting
edge, and its entertainment industry became a
combination of familiar, if lavish, music-hall and
tawdry manifestations of the sex industry.

3-SECOND PERSPECTIVE
The Sacré-Cœur
dominates the skyline,
and Montmartre's summit
and music-halls at the
foot of the hill have been
depicted by artists from
the 1880s.

3-MINUTE SOJOURN
Construction of the
Sacré-Cœur, designed
by Paul Abadie, began in
1876 and was completed
in 1914. The basilica, in the
then-fashionable Byzantine
style, was funded by
national subscription in the
aim of 'national salvation'
and asserted the power
of the Church, which was
increasingly vulnerable
under the Third Republic.
As such, it was ferociously
criticized by traditionalists,
aesthetes and the Left,
none of whom, however,
prevented it from
becoming one of the
city's most-visited tourist
attractions.

RELATED TOPICS
See also
THE BELLE ÉPOQUE
page 24

MONTPARNASSE
page 36

HENRI DE TOULOUSE-
LAUTREC
page 86

3-SECOND BIOGRAPHIES
PIERRE-AUGUSTE RENOIR
1841–1919
Painter of the *Bal du Moulin
de la Galette*, depicting
working-class Parisians at
leisure in Montmartre

MISTINGUETT
1875–1956
French music-hall star who was
once the highest-paid female
stage performer in the world

JOSEPHINE BAKER
1906–75
Black American music-hall star.
In a bid to combat racism in the
1950s, she adopted 12 children
of different ethnic backgrounds

30-SECOND TEXT
Nicholas Hewitt

*Writers and artists
gravitated towards
bohemian Montmartre.*

MARAIS

the 30-second city

3-SECOND PERSPECTIVE
Built on marshes, from which its name derives, the Marais district, once home to aristocracy and literati, evokes the spirit of '*vieux Paris*', as is evident from its architecture.

3-MINUTE SOJOURN
One of the most extravagant mansions in Paris, L'Hôtel Salé, completed in 1659 as a home for Pierre Aubert, in Rue de Thorigny, is now home to the Musée Picasso. It contains an outstanding collection of artworks donated to the French Republic by Picasso's heirs in lieu of estate taxes. Thanks to the Department of Historic Monuments, the house was refurbished between 1979 and 1985 by Roland Simounet, who restored the building to its former glory.

Le Marais, in the city's 4th *arrondissement*, has been reinvented many times in a history that spans over five centuries. Place Royale, now Place des Vosges, was part of a building project initiated by Henri IV, inaugurated in 1612. It was the first planned square in Paris and attracted the nobility, who built mansions here. Its aristocratic character changed in the mid-eighteenth century and during the Revolution, with the surrender of the nearby Bastille on 14 July 1789, and the nobility fled. The area escaped 'Haussmannization' in the nineteenth century but was, by the first half of the twentieth century, so squalid, overpopulated and unfashionable that it faced total demolition. It was saved by the French Minister of Culture, André Malraux, in the early 1960s and, in 1965, became Paris's first conservation area. Today, its beautifully renovated buildings attract numerous visitors; there are at least ten museums, several important churches, Hector Guimard's synagogue and various cultural institutions. A trendy and cosmopolitan part of Paris, home especially to Jewish communities, Le Marais has recovered its former appeal. As well as visiting the area's boutiques and bars, tourists flock to the Place des Vosges, Victor Hugo's house, the restored Musée Picasso and the Musée Carnavalet, an outstanding example of Renaissance architecture.

RELATED TOPICS
See also
MEDIEVAL
page 18

HECTOR GUIMARD
page 42

GEORGES-EUGÈNE HAUSSMANN
page 110

POMPIDOU CENTRE
page 126

3-SECOND BIOGRAPHIES
HENRI IV
1553–1610
First Bourbon monarch of France who instigated the creation of Place Royale

VICTOR HUGO
1802–85
Romantic writer who lived in an apartment of 6 Place des Vosges between 1832 and 1848, where he wrote some of his most famous works including a large part of *Les Misérables*

30-SECOND TEXT
Sophie Bostock

Named for its marshes, the historic district of Le Marais is known as 'Old Paris'.

PLACE
DES VOSGES

3ᵉ Arrᵗ

N DES POMPES ET MAGNIFICENCES DV CAROVSEL FAICT EN LA PLACE ROYALLE A PARIS LE V. VI VII DAVRIL.

10 March 1867
Born in Lyon; family moves to Paris in 1880

1882–5
Attends the École des Arts Décoratifs

1885–97
Attends the École des Beaux-Arts but fails to graduate

1893
Designs Hôtel Jassedé and its furniture for a neighbour in the 16th *arrondissement*, where most of his surviving buildings can be found

1894
Visits Victor Horta's Hôtel Tassel (1893) in Brussels

1894–8
Meets the young widow Fournier who commissions the Castel Béranger, a block of 36 flats, now recognized as the beginning of French Art Nouveau architecture

1899–1900
Commissioned by the Paris Métro to design the entrances for their new stations; of those that remain, Porte Dauphine has the most complete structure

1898–1900
Construction of Humbert-de-Romans concert hall using acoustic-enhancing structural innovations; demolished in 1905

1899–1903
Construction of Castel Henriette, Sèvres, a fantastic creation, which provided the backdrop for many films until its demolition in 1969

1903
Presents 'Le Style Guimard' at the International Exhibition on housing in Paris

1904–6
Construction of Hôtel Nozal and its furniture, one of several commissions for the industrialist Léon Nozal

1910–12
Presents Hôtel Guimard as a wedding present to his wife, Adeline Oppenheim; creates new structural forms to reflect the functional demands of the interior layout

1913
Construction of the synagogue in the Marais district with reinforced concrete

1929
Awarded the Legion of Honour

1930
Final construction – he was responsible for around 300 buildings in all – is a house in Vaucresson, whose externalized pipework serves both structural and decorative functions

20 May 1942
Dies in New York

1948
Guimard's widow's offer of their private home and furniture to the French state is turned down

1960
Major exhibition on 'Sources of the 20th Century' at the Pompidou Centre marks start of official re-evaluation

1972
Castel Béranger classified as a historical monument

HECTOR GUIMARD

Designer-architect Hector

Guimard provided *fin-de-siècle* Paris with one of its most characteristic features: the distinctive green, cast-iron 'Métropolitain' entrances with their bug-eyed arches, glazed canopies and distinctive typography. These fantastical structures helped to introduce the public to Art Nouveau and to site Paris at the heart of an international movement.

Originally from Lyon, Guimard moved to Paris aged 13, where he attended first the École des Arts Décoratifs (where he was later professsor) and the prestigious École des Beaux-Arts, absorbing the ideas of Eugène Viollet-le-Duc, the influential theorist known for his interpretive 'restorations' of medieval buildings such as Notre-Dame. These rationalist ideas laid the foundation for a new kind of architecture based around organic structures, asymmetry and matching materials to their ideal forms.

Guimard was also profoundly inspired by the signature biomorphic 'whiplash' motifs of Victor Horta's Hôtel Tassel in Brussels, which he visited. Guimard's originality derived from his total design philosophy and new vocabulary of architecture and ornament, especially through the creative deployment of contrasting materials, such as stone, brick, terracotta and iron. 'When I build a house,' he wrote, 'I contemplate the spectacle the universe has given me.'

Guimard's breakthrough came in 1894 with the commission to build a large apartment block in the prosperous suburb of Auteuil, west of Paris. Handed the opportunity to let his imagination run riot, he conceived every external and internal detail, from the curved lines of the cast-iron balustrades to the communal spaces, and from the carved stonework over the entrance to the doorknobs and furniture. The resulting Castel Béranger, or '*Castel dérangé*' ('Crazy castle') as his critics dubbed it, won a competition for best façade, as well as the commission to design the entrances for the new Métro stations, in time to greet the 50 million visitors to the 1900 *Exposition Universelle*. There followed a fertile, ten-year period of private commissions, including a fabulous concert hall, several villas outside Paris and his own home. After the First World War, Guimard adapted his style to the demands of the modern age, experimenting with prefabricated materials such as reinforced concrete.

In 1938, Guimard left for New York with his American wife, dying in obscurity soon after. Part of the reason Guimard's legacy was neglected for so long and so much of his work destroyed was bad timing, for he ended up stranded in the crossfire between the stuffy old guard of tradition and the puritanical avant-garde of modernism.

Nigel Ritchie

BELLEVILLE

the 30-second city

Sandwiched between the Père Lachaise cemetery to the east and the Parc des Buttes-Chaumont to the west, Belleville became part of Paris in 1860, but was previously a rural village whose economy was largely based on vine-growing and later quarrying. The magnificent Parc de Belleville, constructed on the site of the former quarry and opened in 1988, still has vines, though is better known for its stunning views of central Paris. Culturally, the neighbourhood has long been important in different ways. It was once home to archetypally Parisian *guinguettes* and, later, to a music-hall, the Folies-Belleville, where stars like Édith Piaf and Maurice Chevalier performed. It has also made frequent appearances in fiction, film and, especially, music, from Aristide Bruant's song 'Belleville-Ménilmontant' and Django Reinhardt's instrumental 'Belleville' to native rocker Eddy Mitchell's biographical 'Nashville ou Belleville'. The former Folies is now noted for its street art and trendy cafés, as gentrification proceeds apace. With less exorbitant rents, Belleville has been colonized by artists and hipsters (*bobos*). Successive inward migrations over the decades – Russian, Polish and German Jews, Armenians, Greeks, Africans, Chinese – have also provided a rich ethnic mix of cafés, shops, restaurants and market stalls.

3-SECOND PERSPECTIVE
Less visited by tourists than Montmartre but of comparable interest, Belleville is a working-class neighbourhood straddling four *arrondissements* in the northeast of Paris.

3-MINUTE SOJOURN
Despite all the demographic shifts, Belleville retains its associations with nostalgia for a vanishing French working class. Many workers settled here and Belleville was active in the revolution of 1848 and the short-lived Paris Commune of 1871. This radical spirit, coupled with the symbolic weight of past figures from the popular arts such as Aristide Bruant, Jane Avril and Édith Piaf (both women were *Bellevilloises* by birth), accounts for its place among the persistent myths of old Paris, even today.

RELATED TOPICS
See also
MONTMARTRE
page 38

PÈRE LACHAISE CEMETERY
page 74

3-SECOND BIOGRAPHIES
ARISTIDE BRUANT
1851–1925
French singer-songwriter, generally agreed to have been one of the founders of French *chanson*

MAURICE CHEVALIER
1888–1972
Working-class French singer whose international career as the archetypal French charmer ranged from *cafés-concerts* to Hollywood films like *Gigi* (1958)

ÉDITH PIAF
1915–63
Starting her career in the mid-1930s, Piaf became France's most celebrated singing star across the world

30-SECOND TEXT
David Looseley

The bohemian hillside district of Belleville has attracted musicians and artists alike.

LATIN QUARTER

the 30-second city

3-SECOND PERSPECTIVE
The medieval university quarter is the historic academic centre of Paris and is also graced by the Panthéon, where some of the Republic's greatest citizens are buried.

3-MINUTE SOJOURN
The district's reputation for student fractiousness was reasserted in May 1968, when protests against government university policy led to the occupation of the Sorbonne (supported by sympathizers like Sartre), rioting and barricades. Ironically, Boulevard Saint-Michel, originally designed to quell insurrections, became the main battlefield between students and riot police. Student demands were partially met by the fragmentation of the university into more manageable units, although often at the expense of relocation to outlying districts.

On the Montagne Sainte-Geneviève, the highest point on the Left Bank and the site of the forum of Roman Lutetia (the predecessor of present-day Paris), the Latin Quarter, with its parish church of Saint-Étienne-du-Mont, extends between the Seine and the Luxembourg gardens and on either side of Haussmann's Boulevard Saint-Michel. The small theological college founded by Robert de Sorbon in 1253 became the Sorbonne, the centre of the largest medieval university in Europe, with an international student population using Latin as a common language – hence the district's name. With the acquisition in 1469 of the first printing press in France, it became a major publishing centre. The Sorbonne is surrounded by other prestigious institutions: the Collège de France (1530), the Lycée Henri IV (1796) and *grandes écoles*, like the École Polytechnique (1805), now in Palaiseau in the suburbs. The Panthéon, a neo-classical church transformed in 1791 into a national mausoleum for the Republic's heroes, dominates the Left Bank skyline. From its earliest days, the quarter was a vibrant community, with cheap lodgings and taverns, in which the student population coexisted, and often fought, with local traders, criminals and artists, as reflected in the life of medieval poet Villon, and was later the basis for Murger's and Puccini's sentimental depictions of bohemia in nineteenth-century Paris.

RELATED TOPICS
See also
GALLO-ROMAN PARIS
page 16

MEDIEVAL PARIS
page 18

GEORGES-EUGÈNE HAUSSMANN
page 110

3-SECOND BIOGRAPHIES
FRANÇOIS VILLON
1431–c. 1463
Student, criminal and poet, author of *Le Lais* (c. 1456) and *Le Testament* (1461)

HENRI MURGER
1822–61
Poet and novelist, who celebrated bohemian-life Paris, particularly in *Le Pays Latin* (1851) and *Scènes de la vie de bohème* (1847–9), the basis for Puccini's opera *La Bohème*

JEAN-PAUL SARTRE
1905–80
Philosopher, novelist, journalist and playwright who supported the 'events' of May 1968

30-SECOND TEXT
Nicholas Hewitt

The Latin Quarter is Paris's academic centre.

THE SEINE & OPEN SPACES

arrondissement An administrative district with its own council and elected mayor. An initial 12 were created in Paris in 1795 and increased to 20 in 1759 under Napoléon III. They differ in size and population and, in 2016, the mayor, Anne Hildago, proposed a conflation of the first four into a single administrative unit by 2020, though each would retain its number. Lyon and Marseille are the only two other French towns to have numbered *arrondissements*.

beaux quartiers A wealthy residential area principally in the 8th, 16th and 17th *arrondissements* of Paris, backing onto the Bois de Boulogne and populated both by families who have been there for several generations and by *nouveaux riches*. Property is extremely expensive and political affiliation tends to be to the right.

bouquinistes Second-hand booksellers. The word derives from the slang *bouquin* for book. The verb *bouquiner* means both to read and to search for books.

Directory A committee of five that governed France between 1795 and 1799. It tempered the climate of the early years of the Revolution but lacked a consistent political policy, was weakened by coups and finally overthrown by Napoléon.

Exposition Universelle Held in 1889, the universal exhibition, or world fair, was intended to commemorate the beginning of the Revolution and covered nearly a square kilometre of central Paris with its centre on the Champs de Mars.

flâneur Literally a stroller or an idler and male. In the mid-nineteenth century and thereafter, with Haussmann's urban developments, the description broadened to include his sense of observation and curiosity. The *flâneur* was also regarded as an outsider and became symbolic as a distinctive Parisian type.

grands projets An architectural project developed between 1982 and 1998 to symbolize, through major buildings, the preeminence of France in the modern world. The initial idea was conceived by President Valéry Giscard d'Estaing but it was enthusiastically adopted and developed by François Mitterrand. Examples are the new opera house at Bastille, the Ministry of Finance at Bercy and the Grande Arche at La Défense.

hôtel In addition to its normal English meaning, the word can describe a detached private mansion (*hôtel particulier*) and also administrative buildings such as Hôtel de Ville (town hall) or Hôtel des Impôts (tax office).

May 1968 The month when student unrest, massive and violent demonstrations and a general strike caused the downfall of the government and the eventual resignation of General de Gaulle as president.

Memorial of the Deportation Beneath the easternmost tip of the Île de la Cité and almost at water level is the memorial to the thousands of French deported to concentration camps during the Occupation. A stark courtyard containing seven steel stakes fitted with jagged blades fronts a hexagonal chamber studded with tiny lights, bare cells with heavy reinforced doors and on the walls are quotations from works by writers commemorating the Resistance.

Périphérique The Paris ring-road, opened in 1973, is over 35 kilometres (21 miles) long, and almost precisely follows the lines of the walls and fortifications of the capital of the 1870s. Used by nearly a million vehicles per day, it is the source of considerable noise and pollution.

Petite ceinture The nickname ('little belt') given to a railway line running around Paris inside the line followed by the old walls and fortifications and constructed between 1852 and 1869. Initially conceived by the military as a way of transporting troops and material around Paris quickly, it subsequently had urban and commercial uses until the 1970s and fragments continued to be used until the early 2000s. While most is closed with points of access blocked, a few sections (in the 14th, 15th, 16th and 17th *arrondissements*) are officially open to the public and more are planned. With nature having recolonized much of it, it is seen as making a vital contribution to the capital's ecosystem.

RER Réseau Express Régional, the rapid transit system linking city centre and suburbs.

salon A gathering, usually in a well-to-do lady's residence, for intellectual and cultural discussion, popular especially in the eighteenth century. By the nineteenth century, the term was commonly used to describe an exhibition, usually of art.

Second Empire (1852–70) The period under Louis-Napoléon (Napoléon III) that saw a return to a monarchical constitution and a period of colonial expansion. The last ten years were more liberal, Baron Haussmann was appointed to oversee the reconstruction of Paris and commercial enterprises flourished, notably in the creation of department stores. With the defeat of France, Napoléon III was briefly imprisoned in Germany before being exiled in England, where he died in 1873.

BRIDGES

the 30-second city

Thirty-seven bridges (*ponts*) currently span the Seine in central Paris. While the river has been crossed since antiquity at the site of Pont Notre-Dame, today those bridges retaining their original state range from seventeenth-century monuments of the past to contemporary masterpieces of engineering. Pont Neuf, meaning 'new bridge', is actually the oldest standing bridge in Paris (completed in 1607). At the other end of the spectrum is the Passerelle Simone de Beauvoir (2006). Monarchs, saints and battles adorn and lend their names to the constructions, from Sainte Geneviève (patron saint of Paris) to Simone de Beauvoir ('patron saint' of feminism), from the Battle of the Bridge of Arcole (1796) to the Battle of Bir Hakeim (1942). Repeatedly renamed, reflecting loyalties and celebrations across the centuries, these edifices continue to be highlighted as homages to important individuals and events. Perhaps drawn to the ominous yet peaceful waters of the Seine, desperate people have often jumped from Paris's bridges – in real life, fiction and the ambiguous space between – such as Victor Hugo's character Javert in *Les Misérables* (1862). The story of the death mask of the 'inconnue de la Seine' (an unidentified drowning victim) has been continually retold as a myth of the bridges and the water below.

RELATED TOPICS
See also
ISLANDS
page 54

CANAL SAINT-MARTIN
page 56

3-SECOND PERSPECTIVE
The bridges of Paris have a surprisingly turbulent past of death, myth and romance, offering kaleidoscopic viewpoints on the history and development of the city.

3-MINUTE SOJOURN
Paris's bridges possess an irresistible allure for lovers and artists alike. One such twenty-first-century expression saw the proliferation of padlocks being attached to railings of the Pont/Passerelle des Arts, a rather destructive romantic gesture that led to the partial collapse of the bridge in 2014. The bridges have been the focus of films such as the eponymous *Les Amants du Pont-Neuf* (*The Lovers on the Bridge*, 1991) and *Angela* (2005), which features Pont Alexandre III.

3-SECOND BIOGRAPHIES
ANDRÉ-LOUIS GODY
1828–96
A soldier in the Napoléonic wars commemorated by a statue (*Le Zouave*) on a pier of the Pont de l'Alma, which is commonly used as an informal measure of water levels of the Seine

GUILLAUME APOLLINAIRE
1880–1918
French poet, whose work *Le Pont Mirabeau* adorns the bridge of the same name

CHRISTO & JEANNE-CLAUDE
1935– & 1935–2009
Artist couple who wrapped the Pont Neuf in fabric for their 1985 art installation

30-SECOND TEXT
Elizabeth Benjamin

The 37 bridges of Paris have been witness to the city's romantic and often turbulent history.

ISLANDS

the 30-second city

The multitude of natural islands that once formed the primordial swamp of Parisian civilization have amalgamated over time, leaving only two in the city centre: Île de la Cité and Île Saint-Louis. A third, Île aux Cygnes, is artificial, and houses the Statue of Liberty's pint-sized twin sister. Though disproven by recent archaeological finds, the capital's islands – in particular Île de la Cité – are often considered the birthplace of the French nation. The affluent streets of Île Saint-Louis offer quintessential insight into Paris's radical urban planning, its impressive *hôtels particuliers* belying its pastoral beginnings. Beyond the Périphérique, Île de la Jatte is famous for attracting Impressionist painters, as encapsulated by Georges Seurat's pointillist masterpiece *Un Dimanche après-midi à l'Île de la Grande Jatte,*1884–6 (*A Sunday Afternoon on the Island of La Grande Jatte*). The islands of Paris bear the scars of its troubled past, including the claustrophobic Memorial of the Deportation and the now-peaceful Square du Vert-Galant, which has a history of executions – monuments that cap the eastern and western tips of Île de la Cité, respectively. Further down the Seine, two more islands – Île Saint-Germain and Île Seguin – have recently been transformed from military camp and Renault factory into housing, offices, gardens and artistic spaces.

3-SECOND PERSPECTIVE
The Paris we know was once a series of diminutive islands in a marsh, complete with mythical monsters – a far cry from today's bustling metropolis.

3-MINUTE SOJOURN
Île de la Cité has been a major site of French justice for centuries. At one end of it is the ominous Conciergerie, a prison during the Revolution and still used as a court of law today alongside the golden-gated Palais de Justice. Divine justice sits at the other end in the form of the imposing Notre-Dame Cathedral. Between lie other shades of correction: the island is home to the Police Prefecture and the Hôtel-Dieu hospital.

RELATED TOPICS
See also
GALLO-ROMAN PARIS
page 16

BRIDGES
page 54

NOTRE-DAME DE PARIS
page 100

SAINTE-CHAPELLE
page 102

LA DÉFENSE
page 140

3-SECOND BIOGRAPHIES
LOUIS-PHILIPPE I
1773–1850
King of France who installed his ten children on Île de la Jatte

CHARLES BAUDELAIRE
1821–67
Writer, translator, essayist and art critic, resident of Île Saint-Louis

30-SECOND TEXT
Elizabeth Benjamin

Île de la Cité lies at the heart of Paris and is used as a starting point for measuring distance in the capital.

CANAL SAINT-MARTIN

the 30-second city

Connecting the Seine with the Canal de l'Ourq, Canal Saint-Martin was built in 1802 to bring fresh water to cholera-ridden Paris and to transport goods. In 1860, Haussmann covered over its southern stretch as far as République to make the Boulevard Richard-Lenoir, leaving the northern section, bordered by the Quais de Valmy and Jemmapes, an open waterway, with its locks and characteristic high-arched iron bridges. With the canal's traffic, warehouses and factories, and its proximity to the Gare du Nord and Gare de l'Est, a traditional artisanal population developed, which has now all but disappeared. The Hôtel du Nord, the subject of Eugène Dabit's novel (1928) and Marcel Carné's film (1938), has been demolished, with only its façade remaining, a monument to a lost era. The canal has been a prime example of gentrification: its warehouses and industrial buildings have been replaced by loft-style apartments, which have attracted an influx of younger professionals. Its traffic consists mainly of tourist vessels and it has become a popular leisure district: the canal itself, on which the heroine of Jean-Pierre Jeunet's film *Amélie* (2002) skims pebbles, is an important open space in the north of the city, and is now lined with fashionable shops, bars and restaurants.

RELATED TOPICS
See also
PLACE DE LA RÉPUBLIQUE
page 76

GEORGES-EUGÈNE
HAUSSMANN
page 110

3-SECOND BIOGRAPHIES
EUGÈNE DABIT
1898–1936
Socialist writer whose award-winning novel *L'Hôtel du Nord* became a classic of French cinema

MARCEL CARNÉ
1906–96
Director of many highly regarded films, including *Hôtel du Nord*

JEAN-PIERRE JEUNET
1953–
Film director and screenwriter known for black comedies, including *Delicatessen* (1991), and *Amélie* (2002)

30-SECOND TEXT
Nicholas Hewitt

The charming, tree-lined waterway of Canal Saint-Martin runs through a picturesque district of Paris.

3-SECOND PERSPECTIVE
The tree-lined nineteenth-century waterway, running from the Arsenal to La Villette, with the iconic Hôtel du Nord, is a memorial to a now-vanished popular Paris.

3-MINUTE SOJOURN
The interwar novel and film *Hôtel du Nord* celebrate a rosy image of a popular Paris that was already disappearing. While the renovation of the district can be criticized for exiling the original population in favour of a younger, more affluent one, it may also be praised as a largely successful example of urban renewal and the creation of an attractive green corridor between the Seine and the complex surrounding the Bassin de la Villette.

QUAYS

the 30-second city

The historical status of Paris as a river port means that the banks of the Seine and their quays – with bridges and service roads – have loomed large in Parisian life. The *quais* were initially constructed as port infrastructures, but the displacement of shipping to stretches of the Seine outside central Paris meant that they took on new uses and cultural meanings. Many famous residential and official addresses in Paris have traditionally been on the *quais*, such as those surrounding the beautiful Île St Louis, the Quai du Louvre, the Quai d'Orsay (foreign ministry), and the Quai des Orfèvres (Paris police). During the nineteenth century, the *quais* were developed into 'lower' (*berges*) and 'upper' (*quais*) areas: land closest to the river served waterside commerce and transport, while higher pavements and parapets became sites of promenades and retail commerce. For many decades, tourists have known the *quais* in central Paris around Île de la Cité and elsewhere for their famous *bouquinistes*, selling second-hand books and other publications from compact lock-up stalls. One of the *berges* was until 2016 an expressway (*voie*) named after president Georges Pompidou, who controversially opened these historic cultural-commercial areas to high-density traffic.

RELATED TOPIC
See also
ISLANDS
page 54

3-SECOND PERSPECTIVE
The banks of the Seine – and their booksellers – are a magnet for visitors to Paris, and over the centuries, they have been pivotal to the life of the city.

3-MINUTE SOJOURN
Another much-discussed repurposing of the riverside was first implemented by mayor Bertrand Delanoë in 2002 with the 'Paris-Plage' urban beach project, transforming stretches of *berges* into temporary traffic-free spaces for summer sunbathing, festivity and courtship. In 2016, mayor Anne Hidalgo encouraged access with planned pedestrianization of the Right Bank *berges*. Paris-Plage and the *voies sur berge* expressways represent tensions intrinsic to the *quais* between pedestrian and leisure uses of urban space and commerce, motorized transport and industry.

3-SECOND BIOGRAPHIES
GEORGES POMPIDOU
1911–74
Gaullist prime minister (1962–9) and president (1969–74) who accelerated the 'modernization' of Parisian transport infrastructures

BERTRAND DELANOË
1950–
Socialist mayor of Paris (2001–14) who implemented measures to improve the quality of life of Paris's citizens

ANNE HIDALGO
1959–
Socialist mayor of Paris (2014–) who implemented policies to improve the environment in the capital

30-SECOND TEXT
Hugh Dauncey

Lovers, book-lovers and summertime sunbathers find their place on the banks of the Seine.

BOIS DE BOULOGNE
the 30-second city

The Bois de Boulogne was formerly a royal hunting ground with an abbey at Longchamp on the site of the present hippodrome. As a hideout for robbers and brigands, it was also notoriously dangerous for travellers. It remained neglected until 1858, when it was converted into a landscaped park as part of Baron Haussmann's remodelling of Paris under the Second Empire. Taking inspiration from Napoléon III's love for London's green spaces, especially Hyde Park, engineer Jean-Charles Alphand added 95 kilometres (60 miles) of curved paths and alleys, 400,000 trees, countless flowerbeds and two lakes linked by a cascade. By turning it into an undulating, idealized landscape of slopes, groves and islands, he made it a popular haunt for Parisians and a prototype for other city parks. One of its main attractions is the Jardin d'Acclimatation, which once housed a small zoo and a botanical garden and is now an amusement park for children. Adjacent to the Jardin is the Fondation Louis Vuitton, a sleek-looking art museum. Today, the Bois de Boulogne is closely associated with sport, especially tennis and horse racing. Every May, the French Open is held at the Roland Garros Stadium, and every October, Europe's most prestigious flat horse race, the Prix de l'Arc de Triomphe, is held at Longchamp.

3-SECOND PERSPECTIVE
Paris's second largest public park, after the Bois de Vincennes, is located on its western periphery and covers 846 hectares (2,090 acres).

3-MINUTE SOJOURN
The $143 million Fondation Louis Vuitton, designed by architect Frank Gehry in the form of a ship's inflated sails, was opened to the public in 2014. The two-storey, moulded glass and concrete structure with 11 galleries of varying size, was created with specially adapted 3D design software. From 2016–17, its appearance was dramatically transformed into a multi-coloured chequerboard by the addition of translucent cells to the 12 glass-panel 'sails' by conceptual artist Daniel Buren.

RELATED TOPICS
See also
BOIS DE VINCENNES
page 62

PARC MONCEAU & PARC MONTSOURIS
page 68

ROLAND GARROS & THE SERRES D'AUTEUIL
page 146

3-SECOND BIOGRAPHIES
JEAN-CHARLES ALPHAND
1817–91
Leading civil engineer and landscape-architect of the Second Empire. In 1853, Baron Haussmann charged him with redesigning the capital's parks, avenues and gardens as part of his Parisian makeover

ANDRÉ FABRE
1945–
Leading jump jockey turned champion trainer who has won the Prix de l'Arc de Triomphe seven times – more than any other trainer

30-SECOND TEXT
Nigel Ritchie

Within the beautifully landscaped park are a tennis stadium and tracks for horse racing.

BOIS DE VINCENNES

the 30-second city

Like the Bois de Boulogne and Parc Monceau, the Bois de Vincennes was the site of a royal hunting estate around a medieval château. Originally opened to the public by Louis XV in 1731 and containing some *ancien régime* monuments, like the commemorative pyramid, it was designated a public park in 1855 by Napoléon III to serve the working-class districts to the east of Paris. Designed by Jean-Charles Alphand, the architect of most of the Second Empire parks, it was completed in 1865. With four lakes, broad avenues, extensive woodland, a racecourse and arboretum, it covers 995 hectares (nearly 2,500 acres), a tenth of the capital's total area. It also contains the city zoo, which originated with the wild animal displays for the 1931 colonial exhibition, including the landmark 65-metre (213-foot) artificial rock for mountain goats. Largely replacing the menagerie in the Jardin des Plantes, it followed the pioneering Tierpark Hagenbeck in Hamburg in providing a more natural environment, with animals separated from visitors by moats rather than bars and cages. The wood's popular character is reinforced by the annual fair (Foire du Trône), which relocated from the Cours de Vincennes, a location within the city's confines, in 1964, and the theatre complex La Cartoucherie, opened in 1970 by Ariane Mnouchkine.

RELATED TOPICS
See also
BOIS DE BOULOGNE
page 60

PARC MONCEAU & PARC MONTSOURIS
page 68

GEORGES-EUGÈNE HAUSSMANN
page 110

3-SECOND PERSPECTIVE
Serving the populous eastern districts, Paris's largest public park was landscaped under Baron Haussmann during the Second Empire.

3-MINUTE SOJOURN
The park hosted the first Parisian colonial exhibition in 1907, followed by its more controversial successor in 1931. Organized with liberal internationalist aims by Marshal Lyautey, and attempting to avoid accusations of European superiority, it was nevertheless reduced to celebrating predominantly French imperial richness and diversity and was opposed by the Communists and Surrealists, who organized a counter-exhibition celebrating non-Western art. It was nevertheless immensely popular, attracting eight million visitors, using a purpose-built Métro extension.

3-SECOND BIOGRAPHIES
HUBERT LYAUTEY
1854–1934
French general and colonial administrator who served in Indochina and Madagascar before becoming the pioneering Resident-General of Morocco, where he gained a reputation as a modernizer

ARIANE MNOUCHKINE
1939–
French theatre and film director who founded the collective Théâtre du Soleil in 1964. She is the only woman to have received the International Ibsen Award (2009)

30-SECOND TEXT
Nicholas Hewitt

The Bois de Vincennes is a popular 'green lung' for city-dwellers.

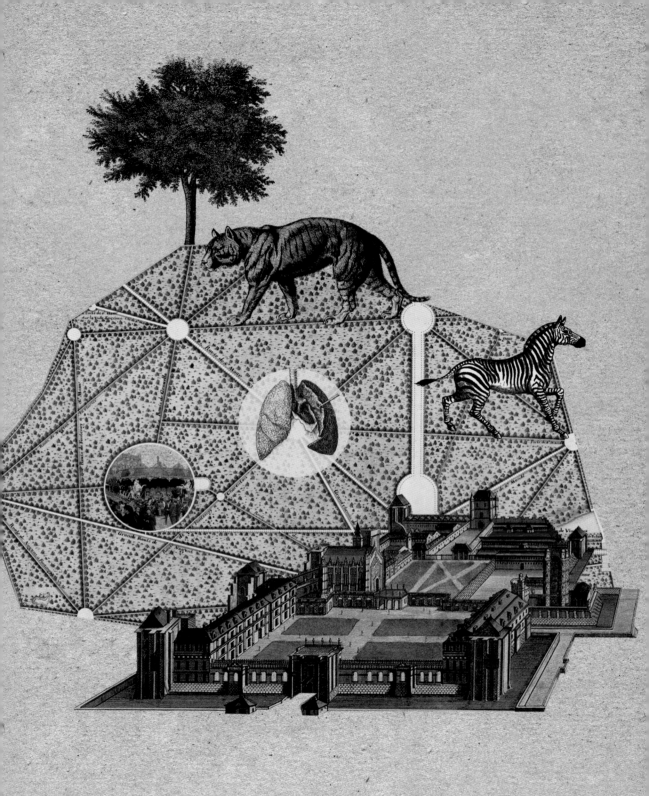

12 November 1840
Born in Paris

1854–7
Studies drawing and painting at the Petite École; fails entry three times to the prestigious École des Beaux-Arts

1863
Takes anatomy courses at the École du Médecine and classes with the animal sculptor Antoine-Louise Barye

1864
The Paris Salon rejects the unfinished *Masque de l'homme au nez cassé* (*Man with the Broken Nose*); Rodin later claimed it as the template for his future work. Meets Rose Beuret who becomes his lifelong partner

1864–70
Works for Albert-Ernest Carrier-Belleuse, a producer of *objets d'art*; produces friezes for several theatres

1871
Moves to Brussels to work with Carrier-Belleuse on the new Stock Exchange; they later collaborate on ornaments for the Sèvres porcelain factory

1875
Visits Italy to study the work of Donatello and Michelangelo

1877
Exhibits plaster version of *L'Age d'airain* (*The Age of Bronze* – originally *The Vanquished*) in the Paris Salon, whose jury rejects it for being too lifelike

1880–1917
Wins first commission to design *La Porte de l'enfer* (*The Gates of Hell*) for a planned museum of decorative arts

1883
Meets 18-year-old Camille Claudel, who becomes his muse, collaborator and mistress for 15 years, as well as a sculptor in her own right

1885
Wins commission for *Les Bourgeois de Calais* (*The Burghers of Calais*), 1895

1889
Commissioned to produce a monument to Victor Hugo for the Panthéon; invited onto the Paris Salon jury

1891
Commissioned to produce a *Monument to Balzac* (1895), Rodin spends four years developing the concept, which was rejected by the Authors' Society as 'unfinished'

1895
Moves to Meudon, Île-de-France

1900
Gains international fame showing 150 works at the *Exposition Universelle*

1908
Moves to the Hôtel Biron in the 7th *arrondissement* of Paris, which becomes the Musée Rodin after its purchase by the state

17 November 1917
Dies in Meudon

AUGUSTE RODIN

A pioneer of modernism, Rodin's rediscovery of the human face and body as a powerfully expressive form made him the most celebrated and innovative sculptor of the nineteenth century, despite frequent criticism during his lifetime.

Born in a working-class district of Paris, Rodin began his artistic career as a mould-maker and craftsman for a number of commercial studios. His solo career did not take off until his mid-thirties with the exhibition of *L'Age d'airain* (*The Age of Bronze*) in 1877. Despite its initial rejection by the Paris Salon, this remarkable freestanding figure, whose accurate proportions and dynamic quality was considered so lifelike that one critic accused him of casting directly from life, marked a turning point by securing his first public commission and his own studio. Indeed, despite their stylistic differences – Rodin was a modeller rather than a carver and preferred clay to marble – Rodin's uncanny sense for anatomy led to frequent comparisons with Michelangelo.

This commission – *La Porte de l'enfer,* 1880–1917 (*The Gates of Hell*), a large-scale, unfinished group of 186 figures, inspired by Lorenzo Ghiberti's doors for the Florence Baptistery (1452) and based on scenes from the 'Inferno' part of Dante's *Divine Comedy* – was originally intended for a new Museum of Decorative Arts. Many of Rodin's best-known works, such as *Le Penseur* (*The Thinker*), 1904, and *Le Baiser* (*The Kiss*), 1887, were scaled-up spin-offs from this project after the commission was cancelled.

Rodin was a compulsive sketcher from life, often recording the same pose from multiple angles. These drawings were followed by clay models and plaster moulds, which formed the basis for his cast (bronze) and carved (marble) versions. This also helped him to recycle many of the same gestures in other works. His two great themes were human sensuality and the lonely suffering of male genius, with most of his work attempting to convey one or the other, such as *La Danaïde* (1889) or his *Monument à Balzac* (1895). Rejected for being 'unfinished', the latter is now considered his most critically acclaimed work.

By his mid-forties, Rodin was running a highly successful workshop, employing casters, carvers – famous assistants included Camille Claudel and Antoine Bourdelle – and foundries to transform his models into finished sculptures. Rodin's desire to disseminate his work widely led to the production of over 300 bronze versions of *The Kiss*, which rapidly established itself as an iconic image of desire, despite being dismissed by Rodin himself as 'a large sculpted knick-knack following the usual formula'.

Nigel Ritchie

JARDIN DU LUXEMBOURG

the 30-second city

The Luxembourg Garden and Palace were created for Marie de Médicis, Henri IV's widow, in the early seventeenth century. The Garden, modelled on Renaissance ideals of formal and 'English' styles, by Jacques Boyceau and Tommaso Francini, once extended as far as Boulevard Raspail, before Baron Haussmann's 'interventions' chopped off the corners. Today, it covers a more modest 23 hectares (57 acres) of tree-lined alleys, symmetrical parterres and raised terraces radiating out from a central, octagonal basin. Over the years, the Garden has come to accommodate more than 100 statues – a legacy from 1830 – an orchard, an orangery, a bandstand, a puppet theatre and an art gallery, which displayed the royal collection between 1750 and 1780 and, later, the Impressionists. The 'Luco' is a quiet, secluded haven set in the heart of the chic 6th *arrondissement*, where families, *flâneurs* and students like to stroll, read, picnic, romance, sunbathe, play chess and sail model boats. Writers such as Jean-Jacques Rousseau, Gérard de Nerval and Ernest Hemingway have all found inspiration in its grounds. After Marie de Médicis' exile in 1630, the Palace was used by various members of the royal family before becoming a prison and seat of the Directory during the Revolution, and then, finally, the home of the Senate.

RELATED TOPICS
See also
LATIN QUARTER
page 46

GEORGES-EUGÈNE
HAUSSMANN
page 110

3-SECOND PERSPECTIVE
The Luxembourg Garden, or 'le Luco', is the Latin Quarter's 'green lung' and a favourite haunt for Parisians and visitors in search of a tranquil space.

3-MINUTE SOJOURN
Following Henri IV's assassination in 1610, his queen, Marie de Médicis, hired architect Salomon de Brosse to model the Luxembourg Palace on her old home, the Palazzo Pitti in Florence. Completed in 1625, it was enjoyed by her for only five years before she was exiled by her son Louis XIII for meddling in state affairs. Sadly, nothing remains today of the original interiors or commissioned paintings, including the 24 scenes from her life by Peter Paul Rubens, which are now in the Louvre.

3-SECOND BIOGRAPHIES
SALOMON DE BROSSE
1565–1626
Architect who designed the Luxembourg Palace (1615–25), and Louis XIII's hunting lodge (1624–6), which became Louis XIV's palace of Versailles

MARIE DE MEDICIS
1573–1642
Born in Florence, the fabulously wealthy Marie de Médicis was Henri IV's second wife. After his assassination, she assumed the regency until her son Louis XIII came of age

30-SECOND TEXT
Nigel Ritchie

The Luxembourg Garden and its baroque Palace have been the setting for many scenes in literature, famously by novelists Victor Hugo and Henri Murger.

PARC MONCEAU & PARC MONTSOURIS
the 30-second city

On the site of a royal hunting lodge, the Parc Monceau began as an eighteenth-century aristocratic folly, laid out by Philippe d'Orléans as an 'English-style' park, dotted with exotic monuments and a lake. Confiscated by the Republic in 1793, under the Second Empire it was the subject of lavish property speculation, described by Zola in *La Curée*, with grand houses adjoining it. What remained, along with the original architectural eccentricities, was re-designed in 1861 by Jean-Charles Alphand as a public park for the inhabitants of wealthy surrounding districts. Ingloriously, in 1871, several hundred Communards were massacred and buried there. The Parc Montsouris was constructed in 1868, again by Alphand, on a former granite quarry, between the populous Alésia district and the city boundary, over the capital's largest reservoir and criss-crossed by railways: the now-defunct *Petite ceinture* and the Ligne de Seaux (now the RER 'B' Line). The landscaping was imaginative, with an ornamental lake, ambitious tree-planting and a weather observatory in the replica of Tunis's Bardo palace from the 1867 Exhibition. Much-used by the urban population to the south, it is also frequented by the students from the residences of the Cité Universitaire, on Boulevard Jourdan, developed in the 1920s to foster international understanding.

RELATED TOPICS
See also
BELLEVILLE
page 44

BOIS DE BOULOGNE
page 60

BOIS DE VINCENNES
page 62

3-SECOND BIOGRAPHIES
PHILIPPE D'ORLÉANS
1747–93
Cousin of Louis XVI who initially sided with the Revolution and adopted the title Philippe-Egalité, which nonetheless did not save him under the Terror

LOUIS-NAPOLÉON
1808–73
Emperor Napoléon III (1852–70) was influenced by London during exile in the 1830s and 1840s and, once in power, imitated its parks in his reconstruction of Paris

30-SECOND TEXT
Nicholas Hewitt

Parcs Monceau and Montsouris were designed by Jean-Charles Alphand, who laid out most of Paris's parks during the Second Empire.

3-SECOND PERSPECTIVE
These two parks, serving the prosperous '*beaux quartiers*' of the west and the working-class areas of the south, are important examples of nineteenth-century planning policy.

3-MINUTE SOJOURN
Impressed by London's parks during his exile in the 1830s and 1840s, Louis-Napoléon instructed Haussmann to provide similar open spaces at all the cardinal points of the city (Bois de Boulogne, Buttes-Chaumont in Belleville and Bois de Vincennes). Supplemented by smaller public squares in each *arrondissement*, they accompanied the new boulevards and older, more formal open spaces (Tuileries, Champ de Mars, Luxembourg) to mitigate the crowded and unhealthy conditions of an over-populated urban environment.

AVENUE
FERDOUSI

JARDIN DES PLANTES

the 30-second city

RELATED TOPIC
See also
MUSÉE DU QUAI BRANLY
page 130

3-SECOND PERSPECTIVE
The Jardin des Plantes began life as a garden of medicinal plants, a leafy enclave in a *quartier* with a longstanding association with botanical and zoological learning.

3-MINUTE SOJOURN
This corner of the Left Bank has long had a connection with the Islamic world. Close to the Jardin des Plantes is the Grande Mosquée de Paris, the first large mosque in France, built in 1926, and still the seat of Islam in France today. During the Second World War, it was used to shelter numerous North African Jews from Nazi persecution. Elements of Islamic architecture can also be found at the Institut du Monde Arabe (Arab World Institute), opened in 1987 as a means of cementing relations between France and the countries of the Middle East.

The Jardin des Plantes was originally founded in 1626 as a royal medicinal herb garden. Located in the 5th *arrondissement* on the Left Bank, the 24-hectare (59-acre) botanical garden also houses a zoo, formerly the royal menagerie (opened in 1794). Its animals were often used as food for the people of Paris during sieges and revolutions. The appointment in 1739 of Georges Leclerc, later the Comte de Buffon, as head of the royal garden led to its transformation and enlargement into a centre of scientific research with a natural history museum sited on the edge of the park. Buffon remained in his position for 50 years and greatly enhanced contemporary knowledge of the natural sciences through publication of his life's work, the 36-volume *Histoire naturelle, générale et particulière.* Four large greenhouses display a range of plants from numerous climatic zones across the globe, heavily influenced by contact with France's empire. The exotic specimens drew the attention of post-Impressionist painter Henri Rousseau, whose best-known paintings are jungle scenes inspired by his visits to the Jardin des Plantes. The museum continues to be home to a significant scientific research community as well as being a major visitor attraction.

3-SECOND BIOGRAPHIES
GEORGES LOUIS LECLERC, COMTE DE BUFFON
1707–88
French naturalist whose encyclopedic *Histoire naturelle, générale et particulière* anticipated the work of Darwin

ÉTIENNE GEOFFROY SAINT-HILAIRE
1772–1844
First professor of zoology at the Natural History Museum. He developed a classification system based on the body form of vertebrates

JEAN NOUVEL
1945–
Architect awarded the Aga Khan Award for Architecture for his design of the Institut du Monde Arabe

30-SECOND TEXT
Nina Wardleworth

The greenhouses in the Jardin des Plantes house an important botanical collection.

CHAMP DE MARS

the 30-second city

'Here dwells a God!' So wrote the ardently Republican historian Jules Michelet in 1847 in his *Histoire de la Révolution française*, describing a visit to the Champ de Mars. Since 1753, when the École Militaire, founded by Louis XV and built by Ange-Jacques Gabriel, had opened on the southeastern edge of this large grassy field on the Left Bank, it had been used for drills. But the god to which Michelet refers is not Mars the Roman God of War (although the field takes its name from the Campus Martius in Rome), but the spirit of the Revolution. For it was on the Champ de Mars on 14 July 1790 that one of the great revolutionary festivals took place: the Fête de la Fédération. From across France, soldiers, legislators, ordinary citizens and the King came together to pledge allegiance to the new constitution. Such fraternal scenes were not repeated the following year, when, on 17 July, protestors who had gathered at the field to demand the removal of Louis XVI were massacred. In the nineteenth century, the Champ de Mars became a place of recreation, used for horse racing and for staging world fairs. For one such fair, the 1889 *Exposition Universelle*, celebrating the Revolution's centenary, the Eiffel Tower was built, originally as a temporary structure.

3-SECOND PERSPECTIVE
Now a perfectly pleasant park by the Eiffel Tower, this former drill ground saw the best and worst of times during the Revolution.

3-MINUTE SOJOURN
The 14th July 1791 was not the only time crowds gathered on the Champ de Mars in anticipation of a better future. In August 1783, aerostation pioneers the Robert brothers successfully launched from the site the first unmanned hydrogen balloon, to the acclamation of enthusiastic spectators. More recently, utopian ideas have found expression in the Wall of Peace, created by sculptor Clara Halter and architect Jean-Michel Wilmotte, installed in 2000 in front of the École Militaire.

RELATED TOPICS
See also
REVOLUTION & TERROR
page 20

THE BELLE ÉPOQUE
page 24

LES INVALIDES
page 106

3-SECOND BIOGRAPHIES
ANGE-JACQUES GABRIEL
1698–1782
Known for his Palladian style, Gabriel was chief architect on many of the major construction projects undertaken during the reign of Louis XV

GUSTAVE EIFFEL
1832–1923
Founded an engineering company, in 1866, that undertook many major railway works, before winning the tender for the centrepiece of the 1889 *Exposition Universelle* – the iron tower that immortalized his name

30-SECOND TEXT
Emma Bielecki

Originally a drill ground for the military, today Champ de Mars is the perfect place to picnic next to the Eiffel Tower.

PÈRE LACHAISE CEMETERY

the 30-second city

In no other place in Paris can you find such a vast galaxy of national and international figures – many of them artists, musicians, sculptors and writers – whose names and fame have long attracted others who can afford to wait and pay for their own tombs here. The biggest cemetery in central Paris, and named after Louis XIV's confessor, Père François de la Chaise, it was initially designed – like those in Montparnasse and Montmartre – in the early nineteenth century as part of a major programme to rid the capital of the stench and dangers of disease emanating from the dozens of overcrowded smaller cemeteries of individual churches. Vastly enlarged (it is more than twice its original size), Père Lachaise resembles a magnificent park and attracts over a million visitors each year. The tombs, of which there are claimed to be over seventy thousand, are extraordinarily varied, set in different sized plots linked by paved paths and shaded by more than 5000 trees, many over a century old. In addition to flowers, some tombs have messages left on them and some have been kissed and even caressed to the point of being damaged. On the eastern side, Le Mur des Fédérés, which commemorates the 147 *communards* executed and thrown into a pit in 1871, overlooks the burial ground of many prominent figures of the French political and cultural Left.

RELATED TOPICS
See also
MONTPARNASSE
page 36

SAINT-DENIS
page 142

3-SECOND PERSPECTIVE
The sprawling park-like cemetery, first known as the East Cemetery, dominates the 20th *arrondissement*.

3-MINUTE SOJOURN
Oscar Wilde, Frédéric Chopin, Marcel Proust, Honoré de Balzac, Eugène Delacroix, Édith Piaf and, most notably, the American poet and singer Jim Morrison are a mere handful of the celebrities buried in central Paris's biggest cemetery. Since 1963, when the Catholic Church rescinded its original ban on cremation, its ornate crematorium has housed the remains of thousands more.

3-SECOND BIOGRAPHIES
ÉDITH PIAF
1915–63
A prolific cabaret and music-hall singer who was immensely popular in France and abroad, notably in America

JIM MORRISON
1943–71
American poet and singer who achieved cult status as a founder member of the rock band The Doors

30-SECOND TEXT
John Flower

Famed for its graves of the famous and infamous, Père Lachaise is one of the most colourful, evocative and visited cemeteries of Western Europe.

EVGENE DELACROIX

ROSSINI

Honoré
de BALZAC

PLACE DE LA RÉPUBLIQUE
the 30-second city

RELATED TOPICS
See also
BELLEVILLE
page 44

CANAL SAINT-MARTIN
page 56

GEORGES-EUGÈNE
HAUSSMANN
page 110

3-SECOND PERSPECTIVE
Straddling the 3rd, 10th and 11th *arrondissements*, Place de la République has radically shape-shifted, from a traffic-clogged intersection of several significant thoroughfares to an airy pedestrian zone.

3-MINUTE SOJOURN
Place de la République has long been a crossroads for public and private transportation. From 1891 to 1924, the Belleville funicular climbed the incline northeastwards from the square to the crest of Belleville. Nowadays, beneath the Place de la République, five Métro lines criss-cross, rendering the square's sub-terrain one of the urban-rail network's busiest junctions.

The 2011–13 renovation of the Place de la République, during Bertrand Delanoë's mayoralty, reclaimed more than two-thirds of its area from the automobile, renewing its function as a site of leisure and concourse, dismantling the legacy of circulation dating from the Second Empire transformations (1853–70). From the 1850s, Haussmann overhauled the small Place du Château d'Eau (named after Pierre-Simon Girard's fountain, since vanished, which had dominated the square since 1811), cutting through the theatres of Boulevard du Temple to create a grander square at the intersection of the new Boulevards Magenta and Voltaire, and Rue de Turbigo. A military barracks was strategically constructed to subdue political insurrection in these traditionally 'dangerous' working-class districts. Redesignated Place de la République in 1879, and overlooked since 1883 by Léopold and Charles Morice's 'Monument à la République' with its imposing statue of Marianne, the square has long served as a symbolic rallying point for public demonstrations. One of the few Right-Bank flashpoints of the May 1968 student protests, the square's pedestrian-friendly transformation has consolidated its amenability to mass gatherings, from the sombre commemorations of the victims of the 2015 attacks to the March 2016 'Nuit debout' protests against labour-law reforms.

3-SECOND BIOGRAPHIES
AIMÉ-JULES DALOU
1838–1902
Celebrated sculptor and *Communard*-sympathizer. His *Le Triomphe de la République*, originally designed for the Place de la République (but losing out in competition to the Morice brothers' work), now sits in the Place de la Nation

FULGENCE BIENVENÜE
1852–1936
Engineer of the Belleville funicular who oversaw construction of the Paris Métro

30-SECOND TEXT
Niamh Sweeney

Marianne overlooks the newly renovated square, which has long been a meeting point for social protest.

MARKETS ◑

Art Nouveau A style of art and architecture developed in the late nineteenth and early twentieth centuries in reaction to earlier traditional forms. Characterized by the use of colour and flowing forms, it is often inspired by the natural world. The entrances to Guimard's Métro stations are an example.

Belle Époque While also a European phenomenon, the period in France, usually recognized to have been from around 1890 to 1914, was one of massive change – in politics, social movement, technology and all forms of artistic activity – with Paris at its heart. Abruptly ended by the First World War, it was subsequently so named with a sense of nostalgia for a golden age that had disappeared.

daguerreotype A photographic image developed on a sheet of silver-plated copper exposed to light. Louis Daguerre initially collaborated with another French inventor, Joseph Niépce, who had discovered the technique in the 1820s, and, after the latter's death in 1833, continued to experiment and revealed it to the public in 1839. Daguerre's name is commemorated in the Rue Daguerre in the 14th *arrondissement*. Original daguerreotypes today fetch a high price.

départements A numbered territorial division directed by a *préfet*, who is appointed by the government. *Départements* were created in 1790 in metropolitan France and subsequent colonies and overseas territories were also numbered. Regional reorganization from 2016 means that certain administrative duties will be lost by many of the original 96 *départements*.

fin de siècle While this phrase literally means the end of any century, it is normally used to include the first years of the following. In France, it traditionally applies to the end of the nineteenth and beginning of the twentieth centuries, a period generally considered to be characterized by unrest and decadence.

flâneur Literally a stroller or an idler and male. In the mid-nineteenth century and thereafter, with Haussmann's urban developments, the description broadened to include his sense of observation and curiosity. The *flâneur* was also regarded as an outsider and became symbolic as a distinctive Parisian type.

grands boulevards The principal boulevards have been constructed at different times with the purpose of opening up the city centre and providing space for leisurely entertainment. From the end of the eighteenth century, they became the site for many small popular theatres. While other boulevards exist, officially there are only four *grands boulevards*, all of which cross several *arrondissements*: Temple, Montmartre, Madeleine and Beaumarchais.

lithographic techniques Originally invented at the end of the eighteenth century, lithography is a cheap method of printing, and hence of publishing, using a smooth stone or metal plate. It became popular in France from the mid-nineteenth century and colours were steadily introduced into the technique.

marché aux puces Flea market. Thought to have emerged during the second half of the nineteenth century and to have referred especially to old clothes and their harbouring fleas. The English expression 'flea market' is thought to have been a direct copy of the French and was first used in the 1920s.

Nouvelle Vague The 'New Wave' was a reaction against traditional film making in France in the late 1950s and 1960s. Directors concentrated on social and political issues – often a reflection of contemporary events – and used their films to express their personal interpretations and ideological positions.

They also used new techniques such as hand-held cameras and filmed on location and with poor light. Leading exponents included François Truffaut, Eric Rohmer, Jean-Luc Godard and Agnès Varda.

Surrealists An artistic, cultural and intellectual movement that began in the early 1920s. Revolutionary in spirit, it was close to the Communist Party in the late 1920s but had become less influential by the outbreak of the Second World War. André Breton (1896–1966) was its de facto leader producing a first manifesto in 1924.

vide-greniers Car-boot sale. Often little more than a collection of unwanted household items sold on plots in the street rented for the occasion. More organized and in part better-quality sales may be known as *brocantes* or *braderies*.

FLEA MARKETS

the 30-second city

Come the weekend and some

Parisians awake at first light because the best bargains in the Puces de Clignancourt, the flea market in the northern suburb of Saint-Ouen, are to be made at dawn. Later in the day, thousands of visitors will wander about this vast realm of the bizarre – a bric-a-brac where the quirky meets the obsolete. Covering 7 hectares (17 acres), the Marché aux Puces de Saint-Ouen is the biggest of its kind in the world and has been an institution since 1885, offering an integral experience that includes regional restaurants and jazz-musette. The famous Rue des Rosiers is the epicentre of a labyrinth of temptations leading randomly to Marché Malassis (toys, vintage cameras …), Marché Dauphine (retro furniture, ceramics …), or Marché Biron (expensive lighting, unusual objects …). Beware: most sellers are foxy professionals rather than occasional secondhand dealers. For the latter, the mish-mash of the Marché de Vanves in the 14th *arrondissement* is perhaps more recommended, with 'only' 400 merchants spread between Avenues Marc Sangnier and Georges Lafenestre. Observe the opportunists who are either selling fake luxury brands or enticing the public to bet on a fraud game called *bonneteau* played on makeshift boards of cardboard, ready to melt into the crowds as the police approach.

3-SECOND PERSPECTIVE
Bursting with vintage second-hand curios and antique treasures – books, furniture, ceramics, art, clothes – the flea markets of Paris are a year-round feature and those of Saint-Ouen and Porte de Vanves are a time-travel experience.

3-MINUTE SOJOURN
The picturesque Puces can still contain hidden jewels. One morning, in 1989, Marc Pagneux, a specialist of old photography, was walking nonchalantly amongst the *vide-greniers* of Porte de Vanves. For a ridiculously low sum, he bought a black-and-white picture of a certain Mr Huet. It turned out to be the oldest portrait ever taken – back-signed by Louis Daguerre himself in 1837.

RELATED TOPIC
See also
RUE DAGUERRE
page 88

3-SECOND BIOGRAPHIES
EUGÈNE POUBELLE
1831–1907
Administrator who made the dustbin (*la poubelle*) compulsory in Paris in 1884, and drove the second-hand markets to the outskirts, for hygiene's sake

DJANGO REINHARDT
1910–53
Jazz guitarist known for his 'Manouche' technique, despite permanent paralysis of two fingers on his left hand, who sometimes played in the Saint-Ouen bistrots

DUKE OF WESTMINSTER
1951–2016
Gerald Cavendish Grosvenor, the 6th Duke of Westminster, owned two of the most prestigious antiques sections of Saint-Ouen

30-SECOND TEXT
Luis de Miranda

The Paris flea markets remain hugely popular with people hoping to snap up a bargain or uncover a real treasure.

da votre ravissant poisson

il — Merci de votre bon

à. Ici point de carte Nr.

Vénus sur cour

PARC GEORGES-BRASSENS

the 30-second city

Named to commemorate the poet and singer George Brassens, who lived locally and whose statue now presides benignly over it, Parc Georges-Brassens in the 15th *arrondissement* has become a fashionable place for a number of media stars to take their weekend exercise. It occupies the site of what was Paris's largest horse market and slaughterhouse, the Abattoirs de Vaugirard, until it closed in 1975 in response to complaints from local people about the noise and smells. At its entrance is a pair of bronze bulls, which, along with the carved head of a horse and the statue of a butcher carrying a huge side of meat, are reminders of the park's bloody past. At weekends, since 1987, a cobbled area becomes one of the capital's biggest and best second-hand book markets, housed inside the former iron-framed meat-market pavilions. Beyond, the landscaped grounds, covered until the end of the eighteenth century by the extensive Périchot vineyard (vines are still grown), are gardens criss-crossed with paths, a boating lake, thousands of trees and bushes, an area with beehives (and instruction in apiculture and sales of honey), huge beds of medicinal herbs, play spaces for children, a school and facilities for the elderly.

3-SECOND PERSPECTIVE
Formerly the site of a slaughterhouse and market, Parc Georges-Brassens is a prime example of successful adaptation in central Paris.

3-MINUTE SOJOURN
Brassens was officially opened and given its name in 1985 by Jacques Chirac, then mayor of Paris. It is immensely popular with people of all ages, many coming from way beyond the 15th *arrondissement*. Part of the restored *Petite ceinture* railway track makes it possible to walk from Brassens to the Parc André Citröen. Echoing another of the park's former uses, vines in Parc Georges-Brassens produce a small quantity of wine, which is sold by public auction at the town hall and the proceeds used for social projects within the *arrondissement*.

RELATED TOPICS
See also
JARDIN DU LUXEMBOURG
page 66

PARC MONCEAU & PARC MONTSOURIS
page 68

QUAI ANDRÉ CITRÖEN
page 112

BERCY
page 114

3-SECOND BIOGRAPHY
GEORGE BRASSENS
1921–81
Popular singer who set many of his own poems and those of others to music, accompanying them with the guitar

30-SECOND TEXT
John Flower

Smaller than the Jardin du Luxembourg or the parcs Monceau or Montsouris, Brassens, in the 15th arrondissement, remains one of the capital's most popular parks.

24 November 1864
Born in Albi in Tarn, southwest France, the first son of an aristocratic family, the Comte and Comtesse de Toulouse-Lautrec

1882
Moves with his mother to Paris, where he lives in the faubourg Saint-Honoré and studies painting under Bonnat and Cormon

1884
Moves into a studio in the Rue Lepic, in Montmartre

1886
Meets Van Gogh at Cormon's studio

1887
First exhibitions in Paris and Brussels

1891
First advertisements for the Moulin Rouge

1896
With Nabi painters Pierre Bonnard and Edouard Vuillard, paints the backdrop for Jarry's riotous five-act comedy *Ubu Roi* (*King Ubu*). Its (public) dress rehearsal on 9 December was the major social and artistic event of the season

1899
Drastic decline in health due to alcoholism and syphilis and is interned in an asylum in the Paris suburb of Neuilly

9 September 1901
Dies at his mother's home, Château Malromé (Gironde, west France), after leaving Paris severely ill then suffering a stroke in Taussat-les-Bains, near Arcachon

HENRI DE TOULOUSE-LAUTREC

In 1896, Lautrec, together with Bonnard and Vuillard, designed and painted the backdrop for Alfred Jarry's avant-garde play *Ubu Roi* (*King Ubu*), in part a pastiche of *Macbeth*, which satirizes the authoritarian institutions of late nineteenth-century France. The opening, five years before Lautrec's early death, was a major cultural event of the Belle Époque that anticipated modernism and the overturning of cultural rules and conventions. While the play met with a riotous response, it proved to be the high point in a career that brought Lautrec worldwide popular and critical fame.

Lautrec was born in 1864 in Albi, southwest France, and his childhood and adolescence were dogged by ill-health, possibly as a result of his family's inbreeding: his lower limbs were stunted and deformed. Deprived of physical activity, Lautrec developed a talent for drawing, which he cultivated on moving to Paris in 1882, where he studied under the major official painters of the day, Léon Bonnat and Fernand Cormon, both located in Montmartre, which was to become the centre of his world. In his short career, progressively blighted by alcoholism and syphilis, he established himself as the pre-eminent commercial artist of the Belle Époque and as an important painter and draughtsman.

Lautrec is best known for his work as a poster-artist, an art form that, using new lithographic techniques, he almost single-handedly invented and took to the level of high art and made him instantly famous in Paris and beyond. His posters for entertainers like Aristide Bruant, Jane Avril and Yvette Guilbert, and the establishments in which they worked – the Moulin Rouge, the Ambassadeurs and the Divan Japonais – depended upon a sureness of line, a sparing, uncluttered focus on the subject, a deft deployment of lettering and, above all, the use of primary flat colours, which became the stock-in-trade of the Fauves. Influenced also by the Japanese printmaking then in vogue in Paris, they constitute one of the peaks of French Art Nouveau.

Lautrec's drawings and paintings, however, are equally as important as the posters that made his name, and demonstrate not merely his exceptional ability as a draughtsman but also an underlying bleakness and cynicism of vision. The latter undoubtedly stems from his physical incapacity and pain and takes the form of a dispassionate, sometimes cruel, depiction of the victims of the Belle Époque, like the prostitutes pictured in the collection *Elles* or those waiting for *L'Inspection médicale* (*The Medical Inspection*), the portraits of *Rousse* or *Casque d'Or* (*Golden Helmet*) and the down-at-heel café clients in *À la mie* (*At the Café La Mie*). This combination of the exuberance and squalor of *fin-de-siècle* Paris and the technical innovation and skill in its evocation make Lautrec one of the most important and popular figures in modern French art.

Nicholas Hewitt

RUE DAGUERRE

the 30-second city

Street markets in Paris are plentiful, with most *quartiers* having several opening on different days of the week but few, if any, are as colourful, convivial and cosmopolitan as the one in the Rue Daguerre in Montparnasse. Running between the Avenue Leclerc and the Avenue du Maine it was originally a simple path becoming known as the Rue de la Pépinière in 1840 in reference to a local nursery before being rebaptized 20 years later to celebrate the work of pioneer photographer Louis Daguerre. Part of today's market in the pedestrian section of the street between the Avenue Leclerc and the Rue Boulard was covered until a building programme caused it to be demolished in the early 1990s. Shops selling high-quality and beautifully presented produce now share the space with several restaurants that have been run by the same families for generations. President Mitterrand returned regularly to one of them to have his driver collect sandwiches that had been specially made for him. Beyond, towards Avenue du Maine, are furniture and accordion repairers, a picture framer, hairdressers and opticians, and the former studio and house of the film director Agnès Varda.

RELATED TOPIC
See also
MONTMARTRE
page 38

3-SECOND PERSPECTIVE
Of the hundred or so street markets in Paris, the Rue Daguerre is one of the smallest but also one of the best, and a magnet for food lovers.

3-MINUTE SOJOURN
In 1976, Agnès Varda made a documentary, *Daguerreotypes*, featuring a stretch of the Rue Daguerre, which had been her home for five decades. It was an intimate portrayal of the shopkeepers, and at the time of its release, the film was described as revealing a way of life that no longer exists. Remarkably, the market has largely survived: Daguerre remains a real village. Several of the shopkeepers' families are interrelated by marriage and local people have shopped here for decades.

3-SECOND BIOGRAPHIES
LOUIS DAGUERRE
1787–1851
Credited, with Joseph Niépce, for inventing photography and noted especially for his invention of the daguerreotype

AGNÈS VARDA
1928–
Film director prominent in the *Nouvelle Vague* movement with such films as *Cléo de 5 à 7* (1962)

30-SECOND TEXT
John Flower

Among the delights along the Rue Daguerre are restaurants, wine stores, a florist and a honey specialist.

COVERED PASSAGES (*GALERIES*)

the 30-second city

RELATED TOPIC
See also
DEPARTMENT STORES
page 94

These glass-covered passages

date from the 1790s, though most were built between 1800 and 1850. Designed to entice in pedestrians to spend their money protected from the weather, noise and dirt of the streets, they were devoted to specialist trades like writing materials and lithography; some also contained fashionable cafés, restaurants, tailors, hairdressers, even hotels, baths and brothels. Constructed to connect two or more thoroughfares, they provided covered pedestrian routes across the city. At their height, there were over 100 such passages, almost exclusively on the Right Bank and clustered around the *grands boulevards* and the Boulevard Sébastapol, while stretching to the Bourse and the Louvre. Privately owned, they were the first thoroughfares to benefit from gas lighting, spearheading the city's drive to modernity. Most were demolished under successive modernization programmes and only about 25 survive, ranging from the earliest, Passage du Caire (1799) and the Passage des Panoramas (1800) to the later Passage Verdeau (1847) and the restored Passage des Princes (originally 1860). Their character varies between chic (Vivienne, Véro-Dodat), more rundown (Passage Choiseul), epicurean 'Little India' (Passage Brady) and eye-catching (Passage Jouffroy houses the Musée Grévin waxworks).

3-SECOND PERSPECTIVE
Ancestors of modern shopping-malls, these early arcades were also secret covered passageways through the Right Bank and an invitation to browsing and chance encounters.

3-MINUTE SOJOURN
In the 1920s, the *galeries* fascinated the Surrealists by their representation of Paris's 'everyday magic', with the often incongruous juxtaposition of bizarre trades and vulnerability to profit-driven urban change: the Passage de l'Opéra, evoked in Louis Aragon's *Le Paysan de Paris* (*Paris Peasant*, 1926), was demolished in 1925. Following Aragon, Walter Benjamin's 'Arcades Project' (1927–40) analysed the galleries as central to the public's fascination with commodities that made Paris the 'capital of the nineteenth century'.

3-SECOND BIOGRAPHIES
CHARLES BAUDELAIRE
1821–67
Poet, art critic and one of the most acute observers of Parisian urban change in the mid-nineteenth century

WALTER BENJAMIN
1892–1940
German Jewish philosopher and cultural theorist, best known for *The Work of Art in an Age of Mechanical Reproduction*, *Charles Baudelaire: A Lyric Poet in an Age of High Capitalism* and the unfinished Arcades Project.

LOUIS ARAGON
1897–1982
Poet, novelist and journalist, who moved from Surrealism to senior membership of the French Communist Party

30-SECOND TEXT
Nicholas Hewitt

Perfect for dedicated flâneurs like Baudelaire, Galerie Vivienne offers idle window-shopping at its best.

PHILATELIE
LA POSTALE
BISTRO
DES
PANORAMAS
RESTAURANT
GALERIE VIVIENNE

RUNGIS—LES HALLES

the 30-second city

In 1969, the contemporary world's largest fresh food market moved from its 800-year-old home at Les Halles in the heart of Paris to Rungis, a vast operation that became known as the *déménagement du siècle* (the move of the century). Six kilometres (four miles) south of Paris, Rungis market could constitute a city in its own right; at 232 hectares (573 acres), it occupies an area larger than the Principality of Monaco, employs over 12,000 people and brings in over 1,698,000 tonnes of foodstuffs annually. While buying and selling is wholesale, the market is open to visitors twice a month, attracting over 20,000 casual gourmets annually. The market opens at 1.00am and closes before midday, with guided tours setting off at 4.30am, when the market is already in full swing. Visitors can explore the seven pavilions that respectively sell fish, fruit, vegetables, poultry, flowers, meat and dairy. The stroller will encounter – in a feast for the senses – stalls trading delicacies such as milk-fed veal, Kobe beef and the classic Bresse chicken; exotic foodstuffs like ostrich, zebra and crocodile; and more traditional fare, such as cheese – although, with over 450 varieties available and wheels of cheese weighing in at 100 kilos (220 lb), there is nothing conventional about this display, which constitutes the largest cheese emporium on earth.

RELATED TOPIC
See also
POMPIDOU CENTRE
page 126

3-SECOND PERSPECTIVE
The Marché International de Rungis is the largest wholesale food market in the world.

3-MINUTE SOJOURN
The politically engaged novelist Émile Zola irrevocably entwined food with the Parisian imagination in his 1873 novel *Le Ventre de Paris* (*The Belly of Paris*), set in Les Halles. For Zola, the cast-iron and glass structures of its architect Victor Baltard and the scale of the burgeoning food industry were representative of urban modernity under the Second Empire. Baltard took his inspiration from the Crystal Palace in London, and his design, which comprised 14 pavilions and cost 60 million francs, became the blueprint for covered markets throughout the Western world.

3-SECOND BIOGRAPHIES
VICTOR BALTARD
1805–74
Architect famous for his design of Les Grandes Halles, whose cast-iron and glass pavilions were completed in 1866. The structures were demolished in 1971, except one, Pavillon Baltard, which was dismantled and moved from Paris to Nogent-sur-Marne, where it is now a heritage site and concert hall

ÉMILE ZOLA
1840–1902
French novelist, journalist and playwright. Known for his 'naturalist' style of fiction, and for his newspaper article, 'J'accuse', during the Dreyfus Affair. Zola's political influence was instrumental in the exoneration of army officer Alfred Dreyfus

30-SECOND TEXT
Gillian Jein

A foodie's paradise, the vast Rungis market boasts a huge range of delicacies.

DEPARTMENT STORES

the 30-second city

The rise of the department store occurred in mid-to-late nineteenth century Paris with the founding of iconic *grands magasins* still in operation today such as Le Bon Marché (1838), BHV (1856), Printemps (1865) and Galeries Lafayette (1894), now an international chain. These stores reinvented shopping since consumers could purchase all they wanted/needed – including clothing, cosmetics, perfumes and housewares – from a single, albeit large, store rather than having to shop for different products in specialized boutiques throughout the city. Goods at department stores were presented attractively, and featured in elaborate window displays, for a mostly female clientele. Considered the very first department store, opening in 1838 as 'Au Bon Marché', Le Bon Marché was expanded by Aristide Boucicaut, who took it over in 1863. Signifying Paris's cultural identity as *capitale de la mode*, the four principal major department stores and their architectural splendours – which include the ten-storey Art Nouveau stained-glass cupola of the Great Hall of the Galeries Lafayette and that above the tearoom of Printemps, an official *monument historique* – are popular destinations for modern-day shoppers and tourists, visited at a rate that is on par with other historic Parisian sites such the Eiffel Tower.

RELATED TOPICS
See also
THE BELLE ÉPOQUE
page 24

MODERN PERIOD
page 30

GEORGES-EUGÈNE
HAUSSMANN
page 110

3-SECOND PERSPECTIVE
In the 1800s, the *grands magasins* of Paris transformed retailing into an art form and today they are as unmissable for their architecture as the city's other monuments.

3-MINUTE SOJOURN
Émile Zola portrayed the inner workings of a fictional nineteenth-century Parisian department store in his novel *Au Bonheur des dames* (*The Ladies' Paradise*, 1883), part of his *Rougon-Macquart* series. The titular department store of Zola's novel was based on the real-life Parisian *grand magasin* Le Bon Marché. Zola's *Au Bonheur des dames* was adapted for the screen, with films by Julien Duvivier (silent, 1930), André Cayatte (1943) and the BBC's television series *The Paradise* (2012–13), which is set in the north of England.

3-SECOND BIOGRAPHIES
ARISTIDE BOUCICAUT
1810–77
French entrepreneur credited with inventing the concept of the modern department store with Au Bon Marché

ÉMILE ZOLA
1840–1902
French author whose 1883 'naturalist' novel *Au Bonheur des dames* describes in detail the Parisian department store of his day and how it eclipsed the smaller shops in the city

30-SECOND TEXT
Marcelline Block

The 'Haussmannization' of Paris was closely linked to the rise of large department stores in the latter part of the nineteenth century.

ART & ARCHITECTURE

axe historique An nearly straight perspective of buildings and boulevards, sometimes known as the Triumphal Way, beginning at the Louis XIV statue in the courtyard of the Louvre and ending with the Grande Arche.

chimera Memorably part of the Gothic architectural detailing on Notre-Dame cathedral, chimera, or grotesques, are images of animals made up of different, unrelated parts, commonly the head of a lion, the body of a goat and a serpent's tail.

départements A numbered territorial division directed by a *préfet*, who is appointed by the government. *Départements* were created in 1790 in metropolitan France and subsequent colonies and overseas territories were also numbered. Regional reorganization from 2016 means that certain administrative duties will be lost by many of the original 96 *départements*.

Enlightenment A European-wide intellectual movement that flourished in France in the eighteenth century, often known as the *Siècle des lumières* (Century of Lights). Driven by a belief in reason, it advanced tolerance and freedom and challenged many hitherto accepted values often underpinned by the Catholic Church and the political establishment.

flying buttresses Literally the supports to counteract the outward thrust of heavy walls and roofs. The 'flying' buttress developed as a feature of Gothic architecture and has the form of an arch with its base away from the wall.

Gothic In architecture, the Gothic style evolved throughout Europe from the twelfth century and is illustrated by many cathedrals and churches. Structurally, its prominent characteristics are flying buttresses, pointed arches and rib windows, the latter allowing light to flood a building's interior.

grands projets An architectural project developed between 1982 and 1998 to symbolize, through major buildings, the preeminence of France in the modern world. The initial idea was conceived by President Valéry Giscard d'Estaing but it was enthusiastically adopted and developed by François Mitterrand. Examples are the new opera house at Bastille, the Ministry of Finance at Bercy and the Grande Arche at La Défense.

legal deposit (*dépôt légal*) The legal stipulation that a copy of every book and of some documents and multi-media material published in France must be deposited in the Bibliothèque Nationale (national library).

Modernism From the late nineteenth century, a rejection of all forms of traditional, classical art considered inappropriate in and for a fast-changing and increasingly industrialized world. In architecture, this resulted in practical, functional buildings (both commercial and domestic), often constructed from blocks, dominated by the use of steel and glass, painted white and with little or no decoration. The principal exponent in France was Charles-Edouard Jeanneret (1887–1965), better known as Le Corbusier.

Palais de la Cité Built on the Île de la Cité, this was the residence of kings and nobility between the sixth and fourteenth centuries before becoming largely an administrative centre as the monarchy favoured the palaces of the Louvre and Vincennes. Left in the care of the minister of taxes, the Comte des Cierges, the palace became known as the Conciergerie. During the Revolution, it was used as a prison. With the particular exception of the palace and its magnificent Sainte-Chapelle, the whole complex, substantially rebuilt in the nineteenth century under the direction of architects including Jean-Baptiste Lassus and Eugène-Emmanuel Viollet-le-Duc, is entirely devoted to legal affairs.

Périphérique The Paris ring-road, opened in 1973, is over 35 kilometres (21 miles) long, and almost precisely follows the lines of the walls and fortifications of the capital of the 1870s. Used by nearly a million vehicles per day, it is the source of considerable noise and pollution.

polychromy Different colours used in particular to decorate the walls of churches, notably the interior ones. This practice was fashionable in the Middle Ages but had largely died out by the sixteenth century. The work was carried out by specialists, who had to follow precise and complicated instructions. Time, the elements and shifting religious practices mean that few examples have survived.

Romanesque Commonly known as Norman architecture in England, the Romanesque style is characterized by semi-circular arches for doors and windows, massively thick walls and towers of various forms. The style pre-dates the Gothic and is found throughout Europe in castles and, especially, in churches and medieval monasteries.

NOTRE-DAME DE PARIS

the 30-second city

This great Gothic cathedral, with its dramatic silhouette and Romantic connotations, is, for many, the essence of Paris. It also marks the historic centre of the French capital, standing on the very spot – the Île de la Cité – where Paris was first settled. Construction began around 1160, spurred by the competing Catholic diocese of Saint-Denis, whose own recently completed cathedral had introduced to the world a new architectural style of height, light and openness: Gothic. Notre-Dame's master masons used the same principles, but pushed them to extremes. Thus its walls are up to eight times thinner than those of Romanesque churches; columns and vaulting use the least amount of stone possible; and pointed arches, a quintessential Gothic feature, also support more with less. 'Flying' or detached buttresses probably played their part but no longer survive – those visible today manage rainwater flow. This clever structural combination yielded the tallest nave yet seen in France, rising 33 metres (108 feet). The later west front is rich in symbolism; its spectacular rose window represents the Virgin Mary (and forms a halo for her statue when seen from the original public approach) and the connection between Earth and Heaven, while its three horizontal layers represent the Trinity.

3-SECOND PERSPECTIVE
The cathedral of Our Lady epitomizes not only true Gothic architecture but also how the nineteenth century interpreted that style – the difference is surprisingly subtle.

3-MINUTE SOJOURN
Having suffered both well-meaning interventions and the deliberate iconoclasm of the Revolution, it was a mutilated, decaying cathedral that starred in Victor Hugo's novel *Notre-Dame de Paris* (1831), known to English readers as *The Hunchback of Notre-Dame*. Part of Hugo's campaign to save Paris's vanishing medieval heritage, the book's success led to a 20-year restoration-cum-reinvention of Notre-Dame by architects Jean-Baptiste Lassus and Eugène-Emmanuel Viollet-le-Duc.

RELATED TOPICS
See also
MEDIEVAL PARIS
page 18

ISLANDS
page 54

SAINTE-CHAPELLE
page 102

3-SECOND BIOGRAPHIES
JEAN-BAPTISTE LASSUS
1807–57
Architect who restored many Gothic churches, including Sainte-Chappelle, and built many more in the Revival style

EUGÈNE-EMMANUEL VIOLLET-LE-DUC
1814–79
Principal Gothic Revivalist after Lassus, under whom he trained, though he also sought a modern interpretation of Gothic using contemporary materials and forms

30-SECOND TEXT
Chris Rogers

Fantastical chimera and gargoyles by nineteenth-century architects haunt the Gothic Notre-Dame.

SAINTE-CHAPELLE

the 30-second city

3-SECOND PERSPECTIVE
One of the purest
expressions of ecclesiastical
Gothic to be found in the
city, the Royal Chapel has
most of its original stained
glass still in place.

3-MINUTE SOJOURN
The Gothic style was
constantly evolving. A
century on from Notre-
Dame, the variation
called Rayonnant by later
historians was firmly
in the ascendant. This
focused on increasingly
intricate decoration, which
was applied to walls and
translated into the thin,
curving bar tracery seen
in rose windows, whose
radiating lines inspired the
style's name. Advancing
technology enabled iron
hooks and tie-bars to
be buried in stonework,
providing additional
strength that permitted
even less wall and even
larger windows.

Sainte-Chapelle was designed for Louis IX to showcase the Crown of Thorns he had recently acquired to bolster his legitimacy as a Christian ruler and Holy warrior. Located within the Palais de la Cité complex and so also serving as the Royal Chapel, the building was completed in 1248 – in readiness for Louis' next Crusade against Muslim-held Jerusalem – after no more than seven years' work; an astonishing feat. Commoners were admitted only to a dimly lit, cramped and pillared lower level, but above them, in the spacious, spectacular main chamber, the king, his retinue and the nobility were bathed in multi-coloured light flooding in through stained-glass windows so generous and numerous there appeared to be no walls dividing them. Carved figures and foliage, finished in red, blue and green paint and gold (polychromy), added to the effect. A nineteenth-century restoration is seen as more scholarly than that at Notre-Dame and indeed was intended as a test case. The spire – by Jean-Baptiste Lassus, whose own face can be seen on its sculpture of St Thomas – dates from this time, along with most of the other skyline features and the entrance portals. Louis IX's Seventh Crusade was ultimately a failure, but this great, glittering reliquary is its legacy.

RELATED TOPICS
See also
MEDIEVAL
page 18

ISLANDS
page 54

NOTRE-DAME DE PARIS
page 100

3-SECOND BIOGRAPHIES
LOUIS IX
1214–70
This king of the Capet dynasty
combined an authoritarian
religious rule with societal
reforms. He died in Tunisia on
the Eighth Crusade

CHARLES VIII
1470–98
An aggressive and expansionist
king who had the rose window
of Sainte-Chapelle rebuilt in
Flamboyant or flaming Gothic,
one of its last variants

30-SECOND TEXT
Chris Rogers

The highlight of this Gothic masterpiece is its magnificent array of stained-glass windows.

ARC DE TRIOMPHE & AVENUE DES CHAMPS-ÉLYSÉES

the 30-second city

Dominating western Paris, the Arc de Triomphe epitomizes the ambition and power of the man who commissioned it: Napoléon Bonaparte. Associating himself with both the ancient Romans and the Sun King (Louis XIV), who erected similar edifices, the Emperor planned this immense arch to be the world's tallest. Begun in 1806 on Napoléon's birthday but not finished until after his death, Jean-François-Thérèse Chalgrin's design is a four-gated monument with an arched passageway in each face. The rich sculptural embellishment includes symbols of military might and vast relief panels celebrating the Revolution and Napoleonic glories. More sombrely, the Great War saw the Arc permanently redefined as a focus of nationhood and mourning and the route through it was blocked by the Tomb of the Unknown Soldier. The Arc initially stood in open countryside, but Napoléon III's later expansion of Paris increased the number of avenues radiating from the Arc to 12, more than justifying the junction's name of Place de l'Étoile ('star'). The broadest remained the Avenue des Champs-Élysées ('Elysian Fields'), piercing the Arc's main axis and extending nearly two kilometres east towards the city centre. First laid out as royal gardens, it soon became lined with luxury hotels and shops.

3-SECOND PERSPECTIVE

A stupendous stone arch, echoing those used for victory parades in antiquity, aggrandizes one of France's most notable leaders and bestrides an equally impressive boulevard.

3-MINUTE SOJOURN

The Arc and the Avenue are part of the 'axe historique', a 10-kilometre (6-mile) sequence of buildings, roads and structures that are exactly aligned. It begins at the smaller Arc du Carrousel, also ordered by Napoléon, in the Louvre's western courtyard. The Place de la Concorde and its obelisk continue the route towards Napoléon's great Arc, cresting the Chaillot hill. Beyond, the Grande Arche de la Défense (1989) outdoes even this architectural colossus.

RELATED TOPICS

See also
MUSÉE DU LOUVRE
page 124

LA DÉFENSE
page 140

LOUIS XIV
page 144

3-SECOND BIOGRAPHIES

FRANÇOIS RUDE
1784–1855
French sculptor whose dramatic *Le Départ des volontaires de 1792* is the most famous of the Arc's carved panels

JAKOB IGNAZ HITTORFF
1792–1867
Architect educated and trained in Germany and France who designed the current setting for the Arc, including the surrounding buildings, in the mid-nineteenth century

30-SECOND TEXT

Chris Rogers

The arch is the focal point where 12 avenues, including Avenue des Champs-Élysées, meet to form a 'star'.

LES INVALIDES

the 30-second city

Begun in 1676, this vast complex was commissioned by Louis XIV as a care home for military veterans. Architect Libéral Bruant borrowed the concept of multiple courtyards formed by long wings from Spain's similar El Escorial to create facilities for 3,000 officers and enlisted men. Plentiful toilets, 'accessible' staircases and sub-divided dormitories set new standards, even if the overall effect was somewhat monastic. Concerns over delays eventually saw Bruant replaced by the younger Jules Hardouin-Mansart, who initially followed Bruant's style, with a tall, aisled nave in Classical garb for the residents' portion of the chapel. More original, however, was his attaching of the necessary royal enclosure in the very different form of a centrally planned church, based on a Greek cross and signalled by an immense dome. The latter's structural ingenuity day-lit Charles de La Fosse's allegorical painting honouring the king, while the articulation of its gilded exterior played with architectural expectations. The shared altar was contained within an oval space that linked the two sections; a century later, Louis Visconti excavated a crypt here to house Napoléon Bonaparte's extraordinary red quartzite sarcophagus, itself a nod to the pomp of Imperial Rome's funerary traditions. Museums now occupy many of the wards.

RELATED TOPICS
See also
REVOLUTION & TERROR
page 20

VERSAILLES
page 138

LOUIS XIV
page 144

3-SECOND BIOGRAPHIES
CHARLES DE LA FOSSE
1636–1716
Paris-born court painter, taught by royal favourite Charles Le Brun, who worked in Britain as well as France

JULES HARDOUIN-MANSART
1646–1708
Great-nephew of the architect after whom the steeply sloped *mansard* roof is named

LOUIS VISCONTI
1791–1853
Architect who also worked for Napoléon III on the Louvre

30-SECOND TEXT
Chris Rogers

3-SECOND PERSPECTIVE
A lavish Baroque pile for wounded and homeless soldiers, completed in 1706, helped glorify one absolutist ruler before becoming the last resting place of another.

3-MINUTE SOJOURN
Louis XIV appeared to care deeply about the fate of the men who had fought for France, which was fitting given how often he himself would wage war throughout his long reign. He personally approved the design of Les Invalides, ensured its increasing budgetary demands were met in the face of sustained opposition from his ministers and lived to attend its opening mass. Les Invalides was also part of the Sun King's extensive arts patronage.

Les Invalides was a home for war veterans, and became Napoléon's last resting place.

BIBLIOTHÈQUE NATIONALE DE FRANCE (BNF)

the 30-second city

Today's National Library (BNF) descends from the private library of Charles V, but its defining mission as guardian of the 'legal deposit' dates from 1537 during the reign of François I. Under Louis XIV, the royal library was systematically developed, and the Revolution enlarged it further, as the now renamed 'national' library acquired the private collections of dispossessed clergy and nobility. In 1868, it moved to palatial new premises on the Rue de Richelieu in central Paris, where it continued growing until, by the 1980s, soaring acquisitions and demand were overwhelming it. In 1988, President Mitterrand announced a personal project to create a 'very big library of an entirely new kind', embracing all forms of knowledge, available to all, and using cutting-edge technologies for conservation and remote access. Accordingly, planners opted to complement the Richelieu site with a stunning new facility at Tolbiac in eastern Paris: an elevated rectangular building housing both a public and a research library and with a glass skyscraper in each corner. Controversies over the new site's architecture, its populist ambitions and the urgency with which Mitterrand was pursuing the whole project, failed to stop the BNF becoming law in 1994.

RELATED TOPIC
See also
REVOLUTION & TERROR
page 20

3-SECOND BIOGRAPHIES
CHARLES V
1338–80
King of France (1364–80)

FRANÇOIS I
1494–1547
King of France (1515–47)

LOUIS XIV
1638–1715
King of France (1643–1715)

30-SECOND TEXT
David Looseley

3-SECOND PERSPECTIVE
As well as the practical duties of preservation and dissemination, the National Library of France (BNF), formerly the Bibliothèque Nationale (BN), serves a deep-seated symbolic purpose.

3-MINUTE SOJOURN
Two decades on, the new facility at Tolbiac is largely accepted, but the initial objections to it, though luddite in some respects, haven't entirely proved misplaced. They heralded today's anxieties about the status of the book – still central to France's identity – in a digital, dematerialized, postmodern culture. Ironically, perhaps, the brash modernism of the four skyscrapers, shaped like open books, is at once a monument to the written word and a symbol of its uncertain future.

The combined sites of the Bibliothèque nationale de France currently hold 14 million books and periodicals alongside many other artefacts, physical and virtual.

27 March 1809
Born in Paris to Nicolas-Valentin Haussmann and Ève-Marie-Henriette-Caroline Dentzel

1831
First appointment as a civil servant, in Poitiers, west-central France

1832–53
Holds a series of positions around France, including promotions to Deputy Prefect and Prefect

1838
Marries Octavie de Laharpe

1840
Birth of daughter Marie Henriette

1843
Birth of daughter Fanny Valentine

1853
Appointed Prefect of the Seine

1857
Awarded honorary title by Napoléon III; Haussmann chooses 'Baron'

1858
On behalf of the city, signs a budget agreement with the state for 180 million francs for phase two of the Paris plan

1869
Dismissed from his post by Napoléon III after refusing to tender his resignation when pressed by the new prime minister

1877–81
Takes up a representative role in Ajaccio, Corsica

1890–3
Publishes three volumes of memoirs

11 January 1891
Dies in Paris; interred at Père Lachaise cemetery

GEORGES-EUGÈNE HAUSSMANN

No individual changed the fabric of Paris more than Georges-Eugène 'Baron' Haussmann, appointed as Prefect of the Seine *département* in 1853 and thereafter responsible for probably the most wide-ranging programme of urban renewal ever carried out in a modern city. Reporting directly to, and working closely with, Napoléon III, Haussmann created new streets lined with elegant apartment blocks, grand civic projects and expansive parks that transformed the capital over the next 20 years.

Haussmann was born in 1809, in the city he would later alter so radically and at a time when society was shifting in ways that would actually make his ascent possible. His family was firmly rooted in post-Revolutionary France – his father and maternal grandfather both served Bonaparte – but in studying law and music, the young Haussmann also reflected the Enlightenment's embrace of rationality and artistry alike.

Haussmann benefited from Bonaparte's modernizations soon after this: division of the country into *départements* provided him his first job and what would become a career in public administration. Steady progress through successive interviews epitomized the values of meritocracy over those of birthright.

Despite having no qualifications in town planning or architecture, the 54-year-old Haussmann demonstrated considerable skill when he finally set about his great task. Beaux-Arts symmetry and Classically inspired rigour, eminently suited to laying out boulevards and squares, were easily swapped for a lyrical Romanticism when creating the parks. Along the new streets, Haussmann allowed designers latitude on the details of buildings even as they worked within strict formulas prescribing heights, depths and form, thus avoiding monotony.

Technology generated by another revolution, the Industrial Revolution, was embraced by Haussmann. Triangulation mapped the, whole of Paris at the outset, stone quarried from beneath it was cut with steam-powered saws, and efficient sanitation, attractive fountains and useful canals tamed the city's waterways.

Neither Napoléon nor Haussmann was prone to sentiment – the latter actually had the very house he was born in demolished – but even Napoléon eventually found it impossible to defend the levels of demolition and disruption necessary to bring about their plan. Haussmann's innovative public–private land deals that helped finance the work were also criticized. Forced to appoint a new prime minister hostile to his Prefect and in the face of sustained political pressure, Napoléon dismissed Haussmann in 1870.

The Empire both men had built collapsed three years later, but 'Haussmannization' continued for decades to come.

Chris Rogers

QUAI ANDRÉ CITROËN

the 30-second city

3-SECOND PERSPECTIVE
The André Citroën complex with the adjoining park is a fine example of imaginative building and landscape design to be found in modern inner-city Paris.

3-MINUTE SOJOURN
The André Citroën development designed in the late 1980s is a striking example of some of the innovative building of the late twentieth century in and around Paris, which includes La Défense, the sports stadium at Bercy and, more recently, the Institut du Monde Arabe, for example. Although, after nearly 40 years, parts inevitably bear the marks of wear and tear, with walls stained by car fumes and even rain, its distinctiveness remains intact.

The spectacular modern buildings with their reflecting glass sides, sharp angles and innovative designs visible from the right bank of the Seine or from the Allée des Cygnes are those of the development built on the site of the former Citroën car and munitions factories, twice heavily bombed by Allied planes in 1944. Thirty metres (100 feet) above ground level, apartments, luxury hotels, shops, cafés, restaurants, multiple sports facilities, a swimming pool and a cinema ensure that residents and even tourists have little need to go elsewhere. The apartments with views across the river are clearly more imaginatively and more expensively designed than those towards the rear but all, around 30 storeys high, are linked by neat paved and well-lit walkways with landscaped bushes, trees and high hedges. As an antidote to the inevitable claustrophobia of such high-density living, there is an emphasis on space, with tower blocks named after stars and planets. To the front of the development, lawns and flower beds form a pleasant and much-needed barrier from the Quai with its incessant stream of traffic making for or coming from the *Périphérique* less than a kilometre away.

RELATED TOPICS
See also
MONTPARNASSE
page 36

LA DÉFENSE
page 140

3-SECOND BIOGRAPHY
ANDRÉ CITROËN
1878–1935
Trained as an engineer and became one of the principal founders of the French car industry

30-SECOND TEXT
John Flower

Once the site of a car and munitions factory, André Citroën is now a much sought-after enclave of chic inner-city dwellings.

BERCY

the 30-second city

The industrial districts of Paris
suffered in the economic downturn of the
1970s. Bercy, situated alongside the Seine and
beyond the medieval tax collection limit, had
been the home of wine storage but was now
struggling. Selected for regeneration as a public–
private development zone, its 40 hectares
(100 acres) next to good transport links have
been utterly transformed. First to emerge, quite
literally, was the half-buried Palais Omnisports
de Paris-Bercy in 1984. Intended as an Olympic
arena adaptable for pop concerts and other
events, its column-free hall has a steel space
frame roof that is supported by four massive
concrete pillars. Sloping sides finished as
lawns make it appear as part of the adjacent
landscaped park, which takes up a third of
the redevelopment site, retains many mature
trees and is split into themed areas. Fringing it
to the north is a sequence of new apartment
blocks, designed by several architects under a
common masterplan. All are broadly U-shaped
around planted courtyards; 'pavilions' in the gap,
separated by bridge-like terraces, give residents
at the rear better views while breaking up the
buildings' bulk when seen from the park. An alley
of original warehouses, preserved, extended
and operated as a food and leisure destination,
buffers the largely glazed commercial and office
buildings encircled by busy rail and roadways.

RELATED TOPICS
See also
MODERN PERIOD
page 30

BELLEVILLE
page 44

QUAYS
page 58

PARC GEORGES-BRASSENS
page 84

3-SECOND BIOGRAPHIES
FRANK GEHRY
1929–
Canadian-American architect
whose Cinémathèque Française
(National Film Archives) at the
western edge of Bercy's
housing epitomizes his
Deconstructivist style

JAQUES CHIRAC
1932–
French politician who served
as prime minister, president
and, from 1977 to 1995,
mayor of Paris

30-SECOND TEXT
Chris Rogers

*The unique architecture
of its sports arena is
one of the highlights of
a regenerated Bercy.*

3-SECOND PERSPECTIVE
Once a neglected symbol
of industrial decay, this
riverside *quartier* has been
revived over decades with
new leisure, residential,
business and cultural
buildings.

3-MINUTE SOJOURN
The revitalized Bercy
site is announced from
the west in the boldest
way possible, with the
extravagant, arresting form
of the Colbert wing of the
Ministère de l'Economie et
des Finances. More than
350 metres (1150 feet)
long, the block bridges a
busy multi-lane highway
and overhangs the Seine
itself, supported by 'legs'
planted in the riverbed.
Completed in 1989 and one
of President Mitterrand's
grands projets, it was
also seen by many as
symbolizing the ministry's
immense power.

MUSEUMS & ENTERTAINMENT

Beaux-Arts An ornamented architectural style based on classical forms and models taught at the École des Beaux-Arts from the last years of Napoléon III's reign to the early years of the following century, when it was increasingly challenged by Modernism and especially by Art Nouveau.

Commune A radical, revolutionary, largely working-class uprising that formed a government in Paris between 18 March and 28 May 1871 during the siege of the capital by the Prussian army and in the wake of the defeat of France and the collapse of the Second Empire in 1870. It was supported by the National Guard, which refused an armistice and was violently suppressed by the Army in May 1871 in a week known as '*la semaine sanglante*'.

experimental music Associated with the Pompidou Centre is IRCAM (Institut de Recherche et Coordination Acoustique/ Musique), an institute for research into sound and music, especially avant-garde electro-acoustic music. It opened in 1977 under the direction of the composer and conductor Pierre Boulez (1925–2016).

Exposition Universelle Held in 1889, the universal exhibition, or world fair, was intended to commemorate the beginning of the Revolution and covered nearly a square kilometre of central Paris with its centre on the Champs de Mars.

fin de siècle While this phrase literally means the end of any century, it is normally used to include the first years of the following. In France, it traditionally applies to the end of the nineteenth and beginning of the twentieth centuries, a period generally considered to be characterized by unrest and decadence.

Franco-Prussian War Fearful of Prussian (north German) territorial expansion, Napoléon III declared war in July 1870. The Prussian forces, who mobilized more quickly than the French, won a number of battles, finally defeating the French at Sédan on 2 May 1871. Napoléon was captured and imprisoned in Germany.

gare French for train station. Paris has six major railway stations serving the provinces and abroad. The Métro and RER (Réseau Eléctrique Régional, the rapid transit system linking city centre and suburbs) line stations are known as *stations*.

grands projets An architectural project developed between 1982 and 1998 to symbolize, through major buildings, the preeminence of France in the modern world. The initial idea was conceived by President Valéry Giscard d'Estaing but it was enthusiastically adopted and developed by François Mitterrand. Examples are the new opera house at Bastille, the Ministry of Finance at Bercy and the Grande Arche at La Défense.

haute couture Luxury, fashionable clothing, especially for women, which began to appear commercially in the late nineteenth century. Increasingly expensive because of the care and time required for *haute couture* garments to be made, the practice waned for much of the twentieth century but was revived as the number of manufacturers increased and regular shows with their catwalks are now held.

May 1968 The month during which student unrest, massive and violent demonstrations and a general strike caused the downfall of the government and the eventual resignation of General de Gaulle as president.

pensionnaires Actors chosen to join the company of the Comédie Française by the theatre's administrator. They are employed by the theatre's general administrative committee and after a year those who remain may be considered as *sociétaires*. Permanent employment, while paid, is not guaranteed and many leave.

sociétaires A selection of *pensionnaires* employed for over a year and elected by the general administrative committee. They enjoy higher salaries, performance fees, a percentage of the theatre's profits, are shareholders and receive a pension.

Théâtre du Vieux Colombier A theatre in the 6th *arrondissement* first established in 1913 by Jacques Copeau (1879–1949). Closed during the First World War, the theatre reopened in 1920 and had a variety of directors until 1975, when, in need of refurbishment, it was restored and listed as an historic monument three years later. Bought by the state in 1986, it eventually became one of the satellite theatres of the Comédie Française.

COMÉDIE FRANÇAISE

the 30-second city

RELATED TOPIC
See also
LOUIS XIV
page 144

The original company was formed when Louis XIV merged the late Molière's troupe with a rival group of actors. The king gave it a royal subsidy and the exclusive right to perform plays in French in Paris. In 1799, it acquired a permanent home on the Rue de Richelieu, where it remains. Napoléon also endowed it with the unusual legal status it enjoys today. On the one hand, it is managed by a general administrator appointed by the French President and receives generous state funding. On the other, its actors – appointed first as *pensionnaires* (probationers), then as *sociétaires* (permanent salaried members) – are effectively shareholders. Another singularity is that several productions run concurrently, alternating throughout the week. They are chosen from a repertoire of over 2,500 works, predominantly classical, though more recently works by modern and non-French playwrights have been added. The establishment trains most of France's best actors, from whom, for the past half-century, its administrators have also been drawn. They have consistently called for a more flexible second venue, to accommodate new approaches to production. The company acquired the historic Théâtre du Vieux Colombier and a new studio theatre in the 1990s, but the proposed Cité du Théâtre in the 17th *arrondissement*, announced by President François Hollande in 2016, aims to realize this ambition fully.

3-SECOND PERSPECTIVE
The mission of France's first national theatre company has remained the same since its creation in 1680: to preserve and reinterpret the greatest works of French drama.

3-MINUTE SOJOURN
As the world's first national theatre, the Comédie Française is uniquely symbolic. It enshrines the French commitment to theatre as a public service essential to citizenship and collective communion. And, as the creature of monarchs, emperors and republicans alike, it embodies the state's concern with the cultural prestige of Paris, even though much of the innovation in French theatre since 1945 has emerged from private theatres or the decentralized public sector.

3-SECOND BIOGRAPHIES
MOLIÈRE
1622–73
Stage name of Jean-Baptiste Poquelin, one of France's greatest dramatists and actors

NAPOLÉON BONAPARTE
1769–1821
French military leader, who was Emperor of France from 1804 to 1814, then again briefly in 1815

FRANÇOIS HOLLANDE
1954–
President of France (2012–17)

30-SECOND TEXT
David Looseley

Where state and culture meet. France's first national theatre has staged plays since the seventeenth century, notably those of the great French dramatist Molière.

CATALOGUE

DE PIÈCES CHOISIES

DU RÉPERTOIRE

DE LA COMÉDIE FRANÇAISE;

*Mis par ordre Alphabétique, avec les Personnages
de chaque Pièce, & le nombre des Lignes
de chaque Rôle, &c.*

GRAND PALAIS & PETIT PALAIS

the 30-second city

3-SECOND PERSPECTIVE
The Grand and Petit Palais are standout examples of *fin-de-siècle* architecture built to showcase French art for the *Exposition Universelle* of 1900.

3-MINUTE SOJOURN
Grand Palais represents the amalgamation of blueprints submitted by four architects who jointly won a competition in 1896 to design the building for the turn-of-the-century *Exposition*. The architects were Henri Deglane, Albert Louvet and Albert Thomas coordinated by Charles Girault, who also designed the Petit Palais. The latter's Classical arches, pillars and Beaux-Arts architecture reflect Girault's eclectic influences. The Grand Palais is still the world's largest steel-and-glass domed structure, London's Crystal Palace having burned down in 1936.

The two Palais were built as part of a new avenue (now Avenue Winston-Churchill) to link the Champs-Élysées via the Pont Alexandre with the Hôtel des Invalides on the southern side of the river. Designed to glorify France's position as a world leader in the arts, the Palais replaced the Palais de l'Industrie (Palace of Industry), which had hosted four previous international exhibitions. The Petit Palais, on the Champs-Élysées, was always intended as an art gallery. Among its extensive permanent exhibits are Greek and Roman antiquities, the art collection of the city of Paris, the largest number of Dutch paintings outside the Louvre, religious icons, Renaissance art, and works by nineteenth-century French masters, including Delacroix, Monet, Sisley, Renoir and Courbet. The Grand Palais, situated between the Champs-Élysées and the Seine, was conceived as a temporary exhibition space under a vast (200-metre/650-foot) span of glass supported by Art Nouveau-style steelwork. Nowadays it hosts around 40 exhibitions annually, including equestrian and other sporting events, car shows, antiques fairs and extravagant fashion shows by *haute couture* houses such as Chanel and Yves Saint Laurent. The west wing is an interactive science museum, the Palais de la Découverte (Palace of Discovery). Substantial renovation in recent years has restored both Palais to their former glory.

RELATED TOPICS
See also
THE BELLE ÉPOQUE
page 24

BRIDGES
page 52

ARC DE TRIOMPHE & AVENUE DES CHAMPS-ÉLYSÉES
page 104

3-SECOND BIOGRAPHIES
EUGÈNE & AUGUSTE DUTUIT
1807–86 & 1810–1902
Brothers whose famous art collection was bequeathed to the City of Paris in 1902 and forms the basis of the Petit Palais' permanent collection

CHARLES-LOUIS GIRAULT
1851–1932
Architect who supervised the work on the Grand Palais and designed the Petit Palais, which served as a model for other commissions in Belgium

30-SECOND TEXT
Sophie Bostock

The Grand Palais and Petit Palais were constructed together with the Eiffel Tower for the International Exhibition of 1900.

ESPLANADE DES INVALIDES

RUE FABERT

DÉCORATION et MOBILIER des HABITATIONS — INDUSTRIES DIVERSES
(SECTION ÉTRANGÈRE)

PONT ALEXANDRE III.

NOUVELLE AVENUE

EXPOSITION DES BEAUX-ARTS

EXPOSITION RÉTROSPECTIVE D'ART

RUE DE CONSTANTINE

PETIT PALAIS

MUSÉE DU LOUVRE

the 30-second city

The Louvre began life as a thick cylindrical dungeon surrounded by towered walls, a fortress built by Philippe Auguste in 1190, of which traces are today uncovered. In the following centuries, multiple transformations occurred, ordered by Catherine de' Medici, Louis XIII and Richelieu: the building became a sumptuously decorated royal palace, until Louis XIV decided to move to Versailles. It was the new French Republic that transformed the abandoned Louvre into a museum in 1793. The Tuileries, now a garden, used to be a part of the residence, but the aisle was burned down during the uprising of the Paris Commune in 1871, opening the breathtaking perspective that now stretches from the Arc du Carrousel to the Arc de Triomphe through the Concorde obelisk. In the 1980s, architect Ieoh Ming Pei was commissioned by President Mitterrand to renovate and expand the Louvre. The result, originally contested because of the glass pyramid that was to serve as the museum's main entrance, is now a landmark of the ensemble. Exhibition areas, which now total 72,735 square metres (782,910 square feet), have almost doubled since the early 1990s; most visitors come to see Leonardo's *Mona Lisa*, the *Venus de Milo*, the mummy Belphegor or Watteau's *L'Embarquement pour Cythère* (*Embarkation for Cythera*).

RELATED TOPIC
See also
LOUIS XIV
page 144

3-SECOND PERSPECTIVE
The most visited museum in the world is itself a metamorphic masterpiece: once a castle, then a palace, it was transformed into a temple for cosmopolitan art during the French Revolution.

3-MINUTE SOJOURN
The history of the *Mona Lisa* is as fascinating as that of the Louvre. The painting was acquired by King François I on Leonardo's death in 1519. Napoléon may have hung it in his private bedroom in the Tuileries Palace. In 1911, the painting was stolen from the Louvre. French poet Apollinaire, who had once called for the Louvre to be burnt down, came under suspicion. Arrested, he implicated his friend Picasso, who was brought in for questioning. In fact the painting was hidden for two years by an Italian employee of the Louvre.

3-SECOND BIOGRAPHIES
PHILIPPE AUGUST
1165–1223
The first King of France, who constructed the original Louvre fortress

PIERRE LESCOT
1515–78
One of the main architects of the Louvre palace, and a master of the French Renaissance

IEOH MING PEI
1917–
Chinese-American architect who renovated and built the new Louvre with its glass-and-steel pyramids

30-SECOND TEXT
Luis de Miranda

The Louvre houses many of the world's masterpieces. To view every exhibit, allowing just 30 seconds for each piece, would take 100 days.

POMPIDOU CENTRE

the 30-second city

Had the revolutionary and rebel spirit embodied in May 1968 been a corporation, its headquarters would be located by the Pompidou Centre. This high-tech structure was built on a parking lot between 1972 and 1977 by architects Renzo Piano, Gianfranco Franchini and Richard Rogers. Their project was preferred over 68 other proposals by President Georges Pompidou, a former literature teacher and also a lover of contemporary art, who thought artists should always 'contest and protest'. Richard Rogers said the idea of putting all the building structure – coloured tubes and disparate scaffolding – on the outside, to maximize the flexibility of the internal space, also had its roots in the volatility of this period of history and its desire for transparency and change. The centre now houses the largest museum for modern art in Europe, attracting some four million visitors every year. It is a who's who of art history since 1905, with works by Picasso, Dali, Matisse, Kandinsky, Warhol and Bourgeois – a total of 56,000 pieces by 5,000 artists. In addition to enjoying its temporary exhibitions, visitors can explore the library, take refreshment on the panoramic upper floor, which displays views over the Paris rooftops, or visit its departments dedicated to art film and experimental music.

RELATED TOPICS
See also
MARAIS
page 40

MUSÉE DU LOUVRE
page 124

3-SECOND BIOGRAPHIES
GEORGES POMPIDOU
1911–74
President of France during the prosperous and agitated years 1969–74

RICHARD ROGERS
1933–
British architect also known for the Millennium Dome and the Lloyd's Building in London

RENZO PIANO
1937–
Italian architect known for his museums commissions and postmodern skyscrapers

GIANFRANCO FRANCHINI
1938–2009
Italian architect who, after the Pompidou project, focused on small-scale cultural projects

30-SECOND TEXT
Luis de Miranda

Iconic modern art and architecture hallmark: the Pompidou Centre.

3-SECOND PERSPECTIVE
The Centre Georges-Pompidou is a 40-year-old act of architectural transparency and a symbol of postmodernism.

3-MINUTE SOJOURN
Equidistant from the Louvre and Notre-Dame cathedral, surrounded by artsy fountains and street performers, the Pompidou Centre was not always appreciated by Parisians, because of its two hectares of gigantic tubes – blue for air conditioning, green for water, yellow for electricity and red for elevators. Also known as Beaubourg – the name of this part of the 4th *arrondissement* – it has various other nicknames, which translate as: 'The Steamer of Culture', 'The Boiler House', 'Notre-Dame of Piping', 'The Oil Refinery' and 'Pompidolium'.

22 October 1844
Born out of wedlock in Paris and raised by her mother before being sent to a convent

1860
Enters the Paris Conservatoire, with the aid of one of her mother's wealthy clients

1862
Joins the Comédie Française but is sacked later that year

1872
Returns to the Comédie Française

1874
Plays Phèdre at the Comédie Française, one of her greatest roles

1875
Becomes a full member (*sociétaire*) of the Comédie Française

1880
Breaks her contract with the Comédie Française. Performs in London and New York

1899
Sets up the Théâtre Sarah-Bernhardt in the centre of Paris

1915
Has her right leg amputated

26 March 1923
Dies in Paris and is buried at the Père Lachaise cemetery

SARAH BERNHARDT

One of the world's most illustrious actors, Sarah Bernhardt was born in Paris in 1844, to a Jewish courtesan and an unknown father. Separated in early childhood from her family and convent-educated, she developed a highly emotional, histrionic temperament that led her to the Paris Conservatoire and, thence, to the Comédie Française at the age of 18. Although she is forever associated with that institution, the relationship between the two was stormy: in 1862, she was sacked from her first appointment and, in 1880, resigned from her second. She was sued accordingly, though by then she had become its most acclaimed actor. But this definitive break proved propitious and lucrative, freeing her to launch her own troupe to conquer London and, especially, New York, where she was an instant hit.

Her signature interpretations were the title roles in Jean Racine's *Phèdre*, Victorien Sardou's *La Tosca* (source of Puccini's opera) and Marguerite in Alexandre Dumas *fils*'s *La Dame aux camélias*. Multi-talented, she was also an accomplished sculptor and painter and even trained as a nurse, tending to the wounded during the Franco-Prussian war (1870–1). Later, she became an actor-manager, most notably at the Théâtre des Nations at Châtelet, which she renamed Théâtre Sarah-Bernhardt (today the Théâtre de la Ville). By 1900, she was a worldwide, if outrageous, celebrity, notorious for her lovers and for sleeping in a coffin. Yet her career began to decline, not least because a knee injury resulted in her having her right leg amputated in 1915. She continued working, though, as well as visiting French troops at the Front and making sound recordings and silent films. Her funeral in 1923 became one of the great moments of public mourning of the twentieth century.

Although she had at times been a victim of French anti-semitism, by her death Sarah Bernhardt had become a national symbol. Her declamatory, emotional acting style – characteristic of the Comédie Française to an extent but nevertheless uniquely her own – was widely applauded. And yet, by 1923, this style, already threatened elsewhere by realism, was also being challenged by a French avant-garde of directors, actors and dramatists who were establishing quite different parameters for the future. Today, perhaps, her primary legacy lies in the blueprint she drew up for the twentieth-century diva, from Garbo to Piaf: melodramatically emotional, wildly creative, vampishly attractive, sexually voracious and internationally adored; a myth created by the imagined identification of her stage roles and her offstage self.

David Looseley

MUSÉE DU QUAI BRANLY

the 30-second city

The museum on the Quai Branly (opened in 2006) was devised as the enduring cultural legacy of the presidency of Jacques Chirac. This followed in the French presidential tradition of Mitterrand's *grands projets* (the Louvre Pyramid, Bastille Opera and National Library, for example) and Pompidou's eponymous art museum. Its collections encompass the arts and social artefacts of the territories of Oceania, Asia, Africa and the Americas. The building itself was designed by the French architect Jean Nouvel. While the museum is known for its innovative displays, such as the musical instrument tower, and the decision to organize its collections thematically, it has been criticized for its overly dark atmosphere, pseudo mud-brick walls and the ambient tribal music, which reinforce stereotypes surrounding non-Western cultures. There also continues to be a reluctance to acknowledge the means by which its artefacts were originally collected during the era of French colonialism. The Quai Branly area houses another of Chirac's legacies, the Memorial to the Algerian War and the Battles in Morocco and Tunisia, inaugurated in 2002 to commemorate France's last and bloodiest war of decolonization. This very modern memorial has a computerized search function to allow families to have the name of their relative displayed on the monument.

RELATED TOPIC
See also
MUSÉE DU LOUVRE
page 124

3-SECOND PERSPECTIVE
Metres from the Eiffel Tower, the Musée du Quai Branly displays a collection curated to celebrate and re-evaluate non-Western art.

3-MINUTE SOJOURN
The garden at Quai Branly has been conceived as an integral part of the museum. It aims to represent the flora of the countries from which the museum's artefacts originate and also includes an 800-square-metre (8,600-square-foot) living green wall. Quai Branly brought together the ethnographic collections of the capital's other national museums (the Louvre, the Musée de l'Homme and the former Musée des Arts d'Afrique et d'Océanie). One of the biggest collections of Asian art and artefacts outside Asia is displayed at the Musée Guimet in the 16th *arrondissement*.

3-SECOND BIOGRAPHIES
EDOUARD BRANLY
1844–1940
Nobel-Prize-nominated physicist and inventor commemorated in the name of the road on which the Musée du Quai Branly is located

JACQUES CHIRAC
1932–
President of France (1995–2007) and Mayor of Paris (1977–95). A desire to increase France's influence in the world through soft, cultural power led to Chirac's decision to create a non-Western art museum

JACQUES KERCHACHE
1942–2001
Art collector and critic specializing in the Primitive Arts, he was Chirac's cultural adviser on the Quai Branly project, but died five years before the museum's opening

30-SECOND TEXT
Nina Wardleworth

The museum houses collections from Africa, Asia, Oceania and the Americas.

MUSÉE D'ORSAY

the 30-second city

In what once was the aristocratic district of Paris lies a temple dedicated to the nineteenth-century artistic spirit. Twelve tons of metallic structures, 35,000 square metres (377,000 square feet) of windows for natural light, and a giant golden clock remind us that this used to be the most elegant train station of France, designed in 1900 by Victor Laloux, eleven years after the Eiffel Tower. Between 1939 and 1986, this was the most notorious abandoned building of central Paris, occasionally hosting cinema shootings, avant-garde theatre plays, auction sales, and parties. After nearly ten years of construction, the museum was inaugurated in 1986 by President and art-lover François Mitterrand, as one of his eight *grands projets*. The building is now famous not only for its architectural structure but also for covering in depth the European artistic period between 1848 and 1914. Apart from its collection of Impressionist artists and its post-Impressionist galleries, the museum is also known for its erotic paintings, neoclassical sculptures, symbolist paintings and its Art Nouveau decorative rooms. Those who plot the milestones of art history will make their choice between Manet's *Déjeuner sur l'herbe* (*The Luncheon on the Grass*), Millet's *Angelus*, Van Gogh's *Nuit étoilée sur le Rhône* (*Starry Night Over the Rhône*) and Caillebotte's *Raboteurs de parquet* (*The Floor Planers*).

3-SECOND PERSPECTIVE
Originally (until 1939) a palace-like train station serving southwest France, the Musée d'Orsay is now a hymn to nineteenth-century art and architecture.

3-MINUTE SOJOURN
Orsay has forged a special relationship with the USA. In 1945, American soldiers helped transform the train station into a camp for the return of deported Jews. In 1961, Orson Welles shot his adaptation of Kafka's *The Trial* in the then-abandoned building. Since 2012, a miniature of the Statue of Liberty, made by Bartholdi in 1899, has stood by the entrance to the museum. And a Texan couple recently made the biggest donation ever to the museum.

RELATED TOPICS
See also
MUSÉE DU LOUVRE
page 124

POMPIDOU CENTRE
page 126

3-SECOND BIOGRAPHIES
CHARLES BOUCHER D'ORSAY
1641–1714
Aristocratic member of the parliament of Paris and adviser to the King, he gave his name to the part of Left Bank where the museum was built

VICTOR LALOUX
1850–1937
The French Beaux-Arts architect and teacher who designed the Gare d'Orsay

FRANÇOIS MITTERRAND
1916–96
President of France (1981–95), he inaugurated the Musée d'Orsay and quadrupled the national budget for museums

30-SECOND TEXT
Luis de Miranda

A former gigantic train station, Orsay still manages to display its collections with a sense of solemn intimacy.

AROUND PARIS

arrondissement An administrative district with its own council and elected mayor. An initial 12 were created in Paris in 1795 and increased to 20 in 1759 under Napoléon III. They differ in size and population, and in 2016, the mayor, Anne Hildago, proposed a conflation of the first four into a single administrative unit by 2020, though each would retain its number. Lyon and Marseille are the only two other French towns to have numbered *arrondissements*.

Art Nouveau A style of art and architecture developed in the late nineteenth and early twentieth centuries in reaction to earlier traditional forms. Characterized by the use of colour and flowing forms, it is often inspired by the natural world. The entrances to Guimard's Métro stations are an example.

axe historique An almost straight perspective of buildings and boulevards, sometimes known as the Triumphal Way, beginning at the statue of Louis XIV in the courtyard of the Louvre and ending with the Grande Arche, one of Mitterrand's *grands projets* constructed in 1989, at La Défense. From the Louvre, it passes through the triumphal arch of the Carrousel, crosses the Place de la Concorde, follows the Champs-Élysées and the Avenue de la Grande Armée and on to La Défense.

bande dessinée (BD) Comic book or graphic novel. Widely popular in France, the BD illustrates all kinds of subjects. An international fair is devoted to it each year in Angoulême.

banlieue The suburbs of more prosperous urban centres, often originally the sites of industrial development. While some have slowly become gentrified, others remain deprived and are areas of social and political unrest. *Banlieue rouge* (red) denotes suburbs that have left-wing, often communist, sympathies.

black-blanc-beur Black-white-Arab. *Beur* is backslang for *arabe* and is used in particular for immigrants from North Africa. Intended as a slogan for integration it became particularly popular when the French team won football's World Cup in 1998.

la drague A slang term for 'chatting up' or 'picking up' – predominantly, but not exclusively, a male activity.

Estates-General (*États-généraux*) A general assembly with three bodies: the clergy, the aristocracy and the common people (the peasantry and the bourgeoisie). Unused since the seventeenth century, the assembly was recalled in 1789 by Louis XVI but was quickly deemed undemocratic with the result that with the result that all three bodies were amalgamated as the National Assembly.

exceptionalism The French belief that France's ways of 'doing politics', her language, culture and society are somehow special and distinct and worthy of being defended.

Gobelins tapestry In the mid-fifteenth century, a family of Flemish weavers settled in Paris and quickly developed a major tapestry enterprise. For 30 years from 1662, it was exclusively Louis XIV's supplier not only of tapestries but also of furniture, paintings and works in silver and gold. When it reopened in 1699, its factories in the 13th *arrondissement* produced nothing but tapestries. The Gobelins dyers continue to do business and are responsible to the Ministry of Culture.

Gothic In architecture, the Gothic style evolved throughout Europe from the twelfth century and is illustrated by numerous cathedrals and churches. Structurally, its prominent characteristics are flying buttresses, pointed arches and rib windows, the latter allowing light to flood a building's interior.

intra muros Latin for within the walls. In the context of Paris, it means contained within the capital's 20 *arrondissements*.

Périphérique The Paris ring-road, opened in 1973, is over 35 kilometres (21 miles) long, and almost precisely follows the lines of the walls and fortifications of the capital of the 1870s. Used by nearly a million vehicles per day, it is the source of considerable noise and pollution.

rafles Mass arrests. The most notorious during the Occupation was of 13,000 Jews carried out by French police on 16–17 July 1942. Those arrested were packed into the *vélodrome d'hiver* (cycle stadium) before being sent to Drancy or concentration camps.

ville nouvelle French for new town. From the mid-1960s, a plan to control growing urban development around major cities was introduced. Nine new towns were initially planned with five around Paris.

VERSAILLES

the 30-second city

Grandiosity was Louis XIV's preoccupation when he proclaimed in 1682 that Versailles was to be his principal residence, the 'showcase' of the kingdom and the new location of the royal court, now that the Louvre was abandoned. Materials used in the construction and decoration, for example the famous Gobelins tapestry, or the vast Venetian-like mirrors, were manufactured in France. A combination of Italian architecture and French classical style, the palace has 700 rooms, seven of which were designed to be occupied by Louis, each dedicated to one of the solar system planets and to the respective Roman god. The same ancient mythology inspired the fountains and statues that surround the property. French nobles and highly ranked personalities were summoned to take a room here to impeach any velleity towards independence. The glass-coated reflecting surfaces of the Hall of Mirrors symbolized the all-encompassing royal surveillance and his power over men. Le Nôtre and Colbert were commissioned to design the gardens with as much care as the Château, celebrating geometry and the king's supremacy over nature. In the eighteenth century, the power of Versailles and its royalty faded, until the meeting of the Estates-General in 1789, held in the Château's *Jeu de paume* (tennis court), announced the beginning of the French Revolution.

3-SECOND PERSPECTIVE
A city built in the seventeenth century around self-styled 'Sun King' Louis XIV, Versailles enjoys a privileged setting with the Château as its ostentatious diamond.

3-MINUTE SOJOURN
Writer Tom Wolfe wrote that he knew of only two perfectly unified cities, Las Vegas and Versailles. While the former revolves around the concept of money, the latter emerged from the absolute centralization of power and its delirious incarnation in the person of the 'Sun King'. The aristocracy was also forced to build houses in the vicinity of the Château. The now-inconspicuously elegant heart of Versailles is still today inhabited by upper-class French.

RELATED TOPICS
See also
REVOLUTION & TERROR
page 20

MUSÉE DU LOUVRE
page 124

LOUIS XIV
page 144

3-SECOND BIOGRAPHIES
LOUIS XIV
1638–1715
The self-styled *Roi-Soleil* (Sun King) who reigned for 72 years

MARIE ANTOINETTE
1755–93
The last queen of France, who spent most of her time in the Petit Trianon palace and its rural surroundings near the Château

ANDRÉ LE NÔTRE
1613–1700
Landscape architect whose designs were executed at Versailles on a lavish scale

30-SECOND TEXT
Luis de Miranda

Versailles and its gardens was the temple of 'Sun King' Louis XIV, proclaimed master of men and nature.

LA DÉFENSE

the 30-second city

Located in the Hauts-de-Seine *département* just west of the capital, La Défense marks the culmination of the ten-kilometre-long *axe historique* of Paris (or Triumphal Way). This famous Right Bank route aligns the Louvre, Champs-Élysées, Place de la Concorde, Arc de Triomphe, Avenue de la Grande Armée and Grande Arche de la Défense. Named after the statue *La Défense de Paris*, the business district of La Défense emerged in the late 1950s, with office buildings such as the Esso Tower and the iconic CNIT convention centre replacing shanty housing, factories and even farms. Esplanade de la Défense is bordered by some of France's highest skyscrapers, including the Tour First, Granite and Cœur Défense, but the esplanade is more than a business district. Every year, it hosts cultural events such as the Paris Christmas market, an ice-skating rink and the La Défense jazz festival. The esplanade is also dotted with over 60 outdoor sculptures, and Alexander Calder's *Red Spider* and Joan Miró's *Fantastic Characters* are only two of the impressive pieces on display at the Open Air Museum. But the district's emblematic centrepiece is undoubtedly the Grande Arche de la Défense, an 'open cube' that stands at twice the height of the Arc de Triomphe and whose archway is large enough to accommodate Notre-Dame Cathedral.

3-SECOND PERSPECTIVE
La Défense is the largest central business district in Europe and the site of Paris's most spectacular modern monument, the Grande Arche de la Défense.

3-MINUTE SOJOURN
Commissioned in 1983 by then President François Mitterrand, the Grande Arche de la Défense was built to celebrate the 1989 bicentennial of the French Revolution. Architects Johann-Otto Von Spreckelsen and Paul Andreu conceived this modern triumphal archway to celebrate the triumph of humanity rather than to commemorate military victories. Until its closure in 2010, the Grande Arche's three-storey rooftop was one of the most visited sites in the city, with perspectives allowing the viewer to see the length of the Triumphal Way.

RELATED TOPICS
See also
MODERN PERIOD
page 30

ARC DE TRIOMPHE & AVENUE DES CHAMPS-ÉLYSÉES
page 104

MUSÉE DU LOUVRE
page 124

3-SECOND BIOGRAPHIES
FRANÇOIS MITTERRAND
1916–96
President of France (1981–95) and the Fifth Republic's first socialist president

ALEXANDER CALDER
1898–1976
American sculptor best known for his mobiles, whose delicately poised shapes become animate in response to air currents

JOAN MIRÓ
1893–1983
Catalan artist known for his use of abstract shapes and vibrant colour

30-SECOND TEXT
Gillian Jein

The business district of La Défense is the financial heart of Paris.

SAINT-DENIS

the 30-second city

3-SECOND PERSPECTIVE
Saint-Denis attracts pilgrims and tourists for its twelfth-century cathedral, where kings and queens of France were traditionally buried, and for the ultra-modern sports stadium.

3-MINUTE SOJOURN
Saint-Denis is separated from central Paris by the (in)famous *Périphérique* that forms a divide between the often socio-economically troubled multi-ethnic 'suburbs' and the more prosperous, mono-ethnic *arrondissements*. In 2005, riots erupted in the *département* of Seine-Saint-Denis, protesting urban deprivation and insensitive policing. Saint-Denis itself has mainly avoided such incidents, but occasionally sees isolated expressions of frustration by *banlieue* citizens excluded from the prosperity of Paris and wider France.

Strictly, Saint-Denis is not in Paris *intra muros* but forms part of the surrounding northern suburb or *proche banlieue*. Despite its historically and administratively separate identity, the conurbation is closely bound to Paris by multiple transport links. Throughout the nineteenth and twentieth centuries, amusingly perhaps, for an area renowned for its left-wing politics, Saint-Denis was associated with the Church and France's royal rulers, who until Louis XVIII (1755–1824) were interred in the basilica of Saint-Denis. This abbey church was elevated to cathedral status in 1966, and is architecturally unique in that its choir, in particular, is recognized as probably the first example of the Gothic style. With declining industrial employment in the late twentieth century, Saint-Denis' fortunes suffered, but the presence of the Université Paris VIII and new commercial and administrative activities, as well as the national stadium, has fostered new hope and civic self-respect, although some social problems remain. Created as the centrepiece of France's hosting of the 1998 World Cup, the Stade de France staged the World Cup Final, where France's multi-ethnic *black-blanc-beur* squad defeated Brazil, prompting an outpouring of national pride and self-congratulatory rhetoric about the perceived – though in reality uncertain – success of ethnic integration.

RELATED TOPICS
See also
MEDIEVAL PARIS
page 18

MODERN PERIOD
page 30

3-SECOND BIOGRAPHIES
SAINT DENIS
died c. 250 CE
Martyred first bishop of and then patron saint of Paris

LOUIS XVIII
1755–1824
King and ruler of France under the first and second Restorations of the Monarchy in 1814–15 and from 1815 until his death. From 1824 until its end in 1830, the second Restoration was ruled by Charles X

30-SECOND TEXT
Hugh Dauncey

With its medieval cathedral – the burial place of many kings of France – and modern football stadium, Saint-Denis is a district of contrasts.

16 September 1638
Born in St-Germain-en-
Laye, from the marriage
of Louis XIII with Anne
of Austria

1643
Louis becomes king,
aged four, on the death
of his father

1660
The king marries
Marie-Thérèse of Spain,
Archduchess of Austria

1661
Death of his first minister
and educator, Cardinal
Mazarin. Fouquet,
Superintendent of
Finances, is arrested for
excess of luxury at
Vaux-le-Vicomte

1661–89
Louis builds the
sumptuous palace at
Versailles

1680
Louis creates the
Comédie Française for
Racine and Molière, now
the world's longest-
established national
theatre

1682
The king and his
government move
to Versailles

1683
Secretly marries Madame
de Maintenon after the
death of Marie-Thérèse
of France

1685
The king ends 87 years
of religious tolerance
with the revocation
of the Edict of Nantes.
Catholicism becomes the
only authorized religion
in France. Thousands of
Huguenots, many of
whom were skilled
craftsmen, fled to
England and Holland

1688–97
Nine Years War against a
European-wide collation
led by German Holy
Roman Empire

1 September 1715
Dies in Versailles after
72 years of reign

LOUIS XIV

The self-styled 'Roi-Soleil' was the absolute European monarch. Constantly fearful of attack, he wanted to be seen as a demi-god who would accept no worldly counter-power. His reign helped to lay the foundations of France's influence internationally.

Louis' parents nicknamed him 'Dieudonné' (meaning 'gift of God') because he was born when they had given up hope of having a child. His education, and the governance of France, was the responsibility of the unpopular Cardinal Mazarin, himself educated by the severe Catholic Richelieu. Most historians say the king's childhood was traumatized by the Fronde, a series of civil wars, from 1648 to 1653, meant to undermine the royal power and favour the aristocracy.

When Mazarin died in 1761, Louis XIV decided to rule without a first minister. He demonstrated his will to shine above all by arresting Fouquet, the too-magnificent Superintendent of Finances who had just thrown the most luxurious party of the century at his Château de Vaux-le-Vicomte. The French parliament also lost much of its power. A new civil code, the Code Louis, was promulgated in 1667, and grand construction projects were ordered, chief among them the Château de Versailles, to reinforce the prestige of the kingdom. Although he was not himself an intellectual, preferring hunting, battles and politics, Louis founded artistic and scientific academies, and sponsored play-writers such as Racine and Molière. However he feared treason too much to enjoy Paris: Versailles was to become the sole capital of France; aristocrats had to move there if they wanted to keep their privileges.

All but one of his children born to his first wife, Marie-Thérèse de France, died in infancy. Several other legitimate descendants were born of the king's relationships with his 'favourites', Mademoiselle de la Vallière and Madame de Montespan. Madame de Maintenon, who took care of the king's offspring, always spoke to him as an equal. 'Madame de Maintenon knows how to love. There would be great pleasure in being loved by her', said Louis before he married her secretly after the death of Marie-Thérèse. But military conquest and political unity were more important. The army was modernized, the number of *Mousquetaires* doubled, and a series of successful wars against diverse European nations were fought, creating enemies in Germany, Holland and Spain. In 1685, Louis decided to end 87 years of religious tolerance: the revocation of the Edict of Nantes was an open war against Protestantism and an alliance with Rome. Many Huguenots, part of the economical and intellectual French elite, found refuge in London, Geneva or Amsterdam.

Before 77-year-old Louis died of gangrene, he told the five-year-old future Louis XV: 'Be a peace-loving prince. War is the ruin of peoples!'

Luis de Miranda

ROLAND GARROS & THE SERRES D'AUTEUIL

the 30-second city

Named to commemorate a

French fighter pilot killed in action in 1918, the Roland Garros stadium is internationally known as the venue for the French Open tennis championship, held there every year since 1928. On the very edge of the Bois de Boulogne and surrounded by massive intersections of motorways and the *Périphérique*, the stadium has been much expanded, but it occupies only part of the park originally created in 1761 as one of Paris's four massive botanical gardens. Between 1895 and 1898, five ornate *serres* were designed by Jean Camille Formigé. Their frames, painted turquoise, are made of cast iron and their supporting gritstone walls are decorated with iron masks by Auguste Rodin. The greenhouses overlook lawns and beds of several thousand rare plants and trees and parts of them, temperature controlled, house a collection of more exotic ones. Another *serre* contains palm trees, azaleas and a pond with Japanese carp. Since 1998, the site has been classified as a historic monument. The French Tennis Federation is to develop its share of the park, of which a third was lost in 1968 through road construction. Initially vigorously opposed by ecologists and local residents and by Formigé's descendants, who claim intellectual property rights, the issue has now been settled.

3-SECOND PERSPECTIVE
Although Roland Garros signifies tennis, the *serres* (greenhouses) and gardens are arguably the most attractive of any in France and frequented annually by thousands.

3-MINUTE SOJOURN
Despite the park's proximity to major feed roads, its landscaped gardens, huge greenhouses and the Roland Garros tennis stadium entice the many who come here to either stay or pass beyond to explore the Bois de Boulogne. The structures of the greenhouses uncannily anticipate Guimard's Métro stations, which began to appear in the capital a decade later.

RELATED TOPICS
See also
HECTOR GUIMARD
page 42

AUGUSTE RODIN
page 64

JARDIN DES PLANTES
page 70

3-SECOND BIOGRAPHIES
ROLAND GARROS
1888–1918
French pilot who fought and was killed in the First World War. In 1913, he completed the first flight over the Mediterranean

RAFAEL NADAL
1986–
Spanish tennis player, nicknamed 'The King of Clay', is the youngest to achieve a Career Grand Slam, at the age of 24, and is widely regarded as the greatest clay-court player of his time

30-SECOND TEXT
John Flower

The Roland Garros stadium will rate as one of the most efficient and attractive tennis venues in the world.

DRANCY

the 30-second city

Drancy is a suburb ten kilometres (six miles) northeast from the centre of Paris and is indelibly associated with a notorious detention centre during the Second World War. In 1940, the German occupying forces used a partly completed housing project (the Cité de la Muette) to hold French and British prisoners of war. From 1941, Jews and other 'enemies of the Third Reich' were incarcerated there. In March 1942, the first convoy of Jewish prisoners left Drancy by rail for Auschwitz. Initially, the French authorities were responsible for the day-to-day running of the camp, but in 1943, its administration passed to the German SS under Alois Brunner. By July 1944, 63,000 of the 76,000 Jews deported from France had been transported from Drancy to extermination camps in Poland. At the Liberation of Paris (August 1944), Drancy operated as a detention centre for suspected collaborators. Today, the former camp serves its original intended purpose as a housing estate and, since 2001, it has been officially listed as one of France's protected sites and monuments. In 2012, a museum/education centre opened opposite a 1977 memorial sculpture and a solitary cattle-truck of the type used for deportation. Families of those who passed through Drancy continue to visit the site for commemorative ceremonies.

3-SECOND PERSPECTIVE
The name Drancy will be forever linked with the deportation of Jews from France to the Nazi death camps in Poland.

3-MINUTE SOJOURN
Jews, who were persecuted both by the Vichy regime and the German occupying forces, constituted the majority of Drancy inmates. Thousands were sent there after mass arrests (*rafles*) by French police in Paris in 1941–2. These included 4,000 children, some as young as two, who were forcibly separated from their parents, transferred to Drancy and deported. None returned. On 6 July 1942, over 1,000 *résistants* and other political opponents were deported; only 119 came back.

RELATED TOPIC
See also
OCCUPATION & LIBERATION
page 28

3-SECOND BIOGRAPHIES
ALOIS BRUNNER
1912–2001
Austrian SS officer in charge of Drancy June 1943–August 1944. Sentenced to death *in absentia* in France in 1954 for crimes against humanity

MAX JACOB
1876–1944
French poet, writer and critic who was arrested by the Gestapo and interned at Drancy, where he died

30-SECOND TEXT
David Drake

Drancy is the north-eastern suburb and Second World War camp from which 63,000 Jews and other 'enemies of the Third Reich' were deported to death camps in Poland.

DISNEYLAND PARIS & PARC ASTÉRIX

the 30-second city

More famous than its French rival

Parc Astérix, Disneyland Paris launched in 1992 as Euro-Disneyland, after difficult and lengthy negotiations between the French state and Disney. Located 30 kilometres (19 miles) east of Paris and directly linked by train from the airport at Roissy, in *ville nouvelle* Marne-la-Vallée, this 'American' theme park has led a chequered existence both financially and symbolically, in a country proud of its cultural and social 'exceptionalism'. Although helping regenerate the Marne-la-Vallée region, it has suffered criticism of its 'too American' management practices, and this very visible presence of Disney pop culture in France has seemed something of a cultural Trojan horse. Parc Astérix, opened by French culture minister Jack Lang in 1989, is sited in Plailly, 35 kilometres (22 miles) north of Paris, and offers attractions based on Goscinny and Uderzo's celebrated *bande dessinée* ('*BD*') stories of plucky Gaulish resistance to Roman occupation. Parc Astérix is thus 'European' in its choice of themes, including, in deference to nearby Paris, an attraction celebrating a version of the capital's history. Unlike Disneyland Paris, open all year round, Parc Astérix closes – in a rather traditionally French manner – from November to April.

3-SECOND PERSPECTIVE
Disneyland Paris and Parc Astérix are major visitor attractions outside of Paris that, since the early 1990s, have provided an alternative cultural focus for tourists.

3-MINUTE SOJOURN
During the 1980s, Socialist culture minister Jack Lang controversially modernized definitions of 'culture' to include pop culture such as BD and other hitherto deprecated artefacts and practices. These reclassifications indirectly facilitated initiatives such as Parc Astérix and Disneyland Paris, stimulating France's ailing economy through creative industries' tourism. Despite greater acceptance of pop culture, official France remains wary of US mass culture, and locating theme parks outside central Paris seems as much symbolic as it is practical.

3-SECOND BIOGRAPHIES
RENÉ GOSCINNY
1926–77
Originator and writer of the Astérix series of comic books launched in the 1960s

ALBERT UDERZO
1927–
Collaborator of Goscinny, and illustrator of Astérix

JACK LANG
1939–
Socialist politician, culture minister 1981–6 and 1988–92

30-SECOND TEXT
Hugh Dauncey

For those seeking more popular forms of entertainment, Paris offers two theme parks – Disneyland Paris and Parc Astérix – the latter being more European in flavour.

LA VILLETTE

the 30-second city

For a century after their creation in the 1860s, La Villette was known mainly for its cattle-markets and abattoirs: the area housed a complex of infrastructures supplying the growing city with meat products of all kinds. Like other markets such as Les Halles and Rungis, La Villette was a space of vibrant and bustling proletarian activity, with subcultures and jargons, where the city's primal needs were satisfied in squalor (sounds and smells of slaughter) and style (some buildings were of elegant architecture). In the 1960s, modernization of the facilities foundered, and commercial activities ceased in 1974, leaving an extensive site of some dereliction, which was eventually redeveloped as the Parc de la Villette. The park now provides food for the soul through the Cité des Sciences et de l'Industrie, the Cité de la Musique, the Zénith concert hall and urban greenery. South of the park, towards Place de la Bataille de Stalingrad and the rotonde de la Villette, the large canal basin that helped serve the abattoirs has, since the 2000s, developed into a gentrified residential and cultural zone – the quartier de la Villette – where people see films, hear music, eat, promenade and jog, and indulge in 'la drague'.

3-SECOND PERSPECTIVE
The village La Villette was incorporated into the capital's 19th *arrondissement* in 1859; nowadays, the *parc* and *quartier* de la Villette are favoured sites of leisure.

3-MINUTE SOJOURN
For much of the 1980s and 1990s, the *bassin* and *quartier* de la Villette were run down and insalubrious in places, but their regeneration created a favourite destination for Parisians and tourists. Most recently, in 2016, Place Stalingrad and other open spaces in La Villette became home to encampments of migrants and asylum seekers.

RELATED TOPICS
See also
CANAL SAINT-MARTIN
page 56

RUNGIS–LES HALLES
page 92

30-SECOND TEXT
Hugh Dauncey

Originally renowned for its cattle markets and abbatoirs, the district of La Villette today contains a wealth of cultural attractions, including Europe's largest science museum.

RESOURCES

BOOKS

And the Show Went On: Cultural life in Nazi-Occupied Paris,
Alan Riding
(Duckworth, 2011)

Atget-Paris
Laure Beaumont-Maillet
(American Ed, 2003)

City Secrets Paris: The Essential Insider's Guide
Robert Kahn
(Granta Books, 2014)

DK Eyewitness Travel Guide: Paris
(Dorling Kindersley, 2016)

Eleven Days in August: The Liberation of Paris in 1944
Matthew Cobb
(Simon and Schuster, 2013)

Forever Paris: 25 Walks in the Footsteps of Chanel, Hemingway, Picasso and More
Christina Henry de Tessan
(Chronicle Books, 2012)

How to Read Paris: A Crash Course in Parisian Architecture
Chris Rogers
(Ivy Press, 2016)

The Invention of Paris: A History in Footsteps
Eric Hazan
(Verso Books, 2011)

Paris
Rick Steves, Steve Smith and Gene Openshaw
(Hachette, 2017)

Paris: Biography of a City
Colin Jones
(Allen Lane, 2004)

Paris, Capital of the World
Patrice Higonnet
(Harvard University Press, 2002)

Paris to the Moon
Adam Gopnik
(Random House, 2000)

Paris: The Secret History
Andrew Hussey
(Viking, 2006)

Paris: Secret et Insolite
Rodolphe Trouilleux
(Parigramme, 1996)

Paris at War 1939–1944
David Drake
(Harvard University Press, 2015)

Parisians
Graham Robb
(W. W. Norton, 2010)

Seven Ages of Paris
Alistair Horne
(Macmillan, 2002)

Shakespeare and Company
Krista Halverson and Jeannette Winterson
(Shakespeare and Company, 2016)

Vestiges of the Colonial Empire in France:
Monuments, Museums and Colonial Memories
Robert Aldrich
(Palgrave Macmillan, 2005)

Walks through Lost Paris
Leonard Pitt
(Shoemaker and Hoard, 2006)

World Film Locations: Paris
Edited by Marcelline Block
(Intellect, 2011)

WEBSITES

Websites for the main sites and attractions of Paris
are easily accessed. Here are some interesting and
useful sites for those visiting the city:

Paris Attractions Map
www.visitacity.com/en/paris/attractions-map
Useful map with information on sights and
attractions in Paris.

Paris, a Roman City
www.paris.culture.fr
Lutetia brought to life with 3D reconstructions of the
town and its monuments, including a useful tour of
Gallo-Roman Paris.

Paris by Train
parisbytrain.com/paris-metro/
Guide to using the Paris Métro with downloadable
maps and useful travel tips.

Time Out Paris
www.timeout.com/paris/en
Guide to the best things to do, restaurants, theatres
and nightlife in Paris.

NOTES ON CONTRIBUTORS

EDITOR

John Flower is Emeritus Professor of Twentieth Century French Literature at the University of Kent. He lives in Paris and has published extensively in the UK and in France, with more than 20 single-authored books, 70 articles and invited contributions and a dozen edited volumes. His work covers French literature and culture since the late nineteenth century.

CONTRIBUTORS

Elizabeth Benjamin is a Teaching Associate at the University of Birmingham. Her research sits broadly within nineteenth- to twenty-first-century French and Francophone Studies, with particular interests in the interwar period, interdisciplinarity and cultural memory. Her first monograph, *Dada and Existentialism: The Authenticity of Ambiguity*, was published in 2016.

Emma Bielecki has taught and researched nineteenth-century French literature at King's College London and Oxford University. She lives in London and is currently working on a biography of Vidocq (1775–1857) – thief, fraudster, imposter and Chief of the Paris Police.

Marcelline Block is a professor and writer, whose publications include *World Film Locations: Paris* (2011) with a Korean translation published in 2014; her co-edited volume *French Cinema in Close-up: La vie d'un acteur pour moi* (2015), and her French to English translation of Jean-Pierre Bertin-Maghit's *Propaganda Documentaries in France,*

1940–1944 (2016). She lectured about Paris in Cinema at 92Y TriBeCa, New York City.

Pierre Boisard is a sociologist and researcher at CNRS (Centre national de la recherche scientifique). His main topics are work, employment, innovation and social cohesion. He lives in Paris and has published several books including *Camembert: A National Myth* (2003), *Le Nouvel Âge du travail* (2009) and *La Vie de bistrot* (2013).

Sophie Bostock is Curator of Prints and Drawings at the Orientalist Museum, part of Qatar Museums Authority, Doha. She obtained her PhD in 2010 at the University of Warwick, on the subject of the late drawings of Domenico Tiepolo and formerly worked as Assistant Curator of Prints and Drawings at the Barber Institute of Fine Arts, Birmingham University.

Hugh Dauncey researches French popular culture, with a special interest in sport. One of his focuses is the urban geography – social, economic, cultural and political – of sporting practices. He is writing a monograph entitled *Paris at Play* on the sites of sport in the French capital.

David Drake has lived in London and Paris and taught at universities in both cities. His extensive list of publications on French intellectuals and politics include numerous articles, two monographs and a biography of Sartre, on whom he is an internationally recognized authority. His most recent book is *Paris at War 1939–1944* (2015).

Gillian Jein is Lecturer in French Studies at Bangor University. She writes on the construction of urban space in modern and contemporary French non-fiction and visual art and is the author of *Alternative Modernities in French Travel Writing: Engaging Urban Space in London and New York, 1851–1986* (2016).

Nicholas Hewitt is Professor Emeritus of the University of Nottingham and Editor of *French Cultural Studies*. A specialist in twentieth-century French culture, he is the author and editor of numerous books, including *Céline: A Critical Biography* (1991), *The Cambridge Companion to Modern French Culture* (2003) and *Montmartre: A Cultural History* (2017).

David Looseley is Emeritus Professor of Contemporary French Culture at the University of Leeds. He specializes in the contemporary history of French cultural practices and institutions and has published extensively on theatre, cultural policy and popular music. His most recent book is *Edith Piaf: A Cultural History* (2015).

Luis de Miranda is a published novelist and academic researcher who has spent most of his life in Paris. His books include *L'Être et le néon* (2012), a cultural history of Paris and neon signs, and a novel set in Paris, *Who Killed The Poet?* (2017) .

Nigel Ritchie is a post-graduate researcher at Queen Mary University of London, specializing in media and the French Revolution, who has been published in *French History* and Freiburg University's E-journal on heroism: *helden. heroes. héros* (2016). Prior to that, he studied anthropology, worked as a writer-editor in reference publishing for 15 years and published several single-authored books.

Chris Rogers is an architectural historian and writer and has authored three books, including *How to Read Paris: A Crash Course in Parisian Architecture* (2016, Ivy Press). His work can also be found at www.chrismrogers.net in a series of long-form articles and blog posts.

Niamh Sweeney is completing doctoral research at the Department of French, University College Cork. Her work considers a variety of cultural practices in and about Paris from 1850 to 1920. She has published a number of articles on Haussmannization and Second-Empire Paris, Baudelaire's art criticism, the Paris Métro and the early twentieth-century French avant-garde.

Anthony Ward, formerly Senior Lecturer at the University of Kent, taught European prehistoric and proto-historic archaeology for over 30 years. He is a Fellow of the Society of Antiquaries of London.

Nina Wardleworth is a Teaching Fellow in French at the University of Leeds. Her research interests focus on cultural representations of French colonialism, especially during the Second World War.

INDEX

ACKNOWLEDGEMENTS

AUTHOR ACKNOWLEDGEMENTS

My thanks go first to Stephanie Evans for tracking me down after many years and for suggesting that I take on this book and to Caroline Earle for her attention to detail and for overseeing its publication. As an exercise in concise writing the book has presented a test and I am grateful to all contributors who have reacted so enthusiastically and who have willingly accommodated any amendments I may have proposed. Finally and as ever my thanks go to J. S. and V. for their forbearance and support.

PICTURE CREDITS

The publisher would like to thank the following for permission to reproduce copyright material:

Alamy Stock Photo/Alex Segre: 149TR; Directphoto Collection: 149TC; Everett Collection Historical: 45TR; Granamour Weems Collection: 45C; Timsimages: 149C.
Bundesarchiv: 29C, 29CR, 29T, 29B, 149TL, 149B.
Clipart.com: 21C(BG), 21R, 21BL, 22, 53TL, 63T, 83C, 83B, 144.
Cooper Hewitt: 42.
Flickr/Jean-Pierre Dalbéra: 131T, 131B; Josh Hallett: 125C; Oakenroad: 27B; Vinicius Pinheiro: 151B(BG).
Bibliothèque nationale de France: 9C, 9R, 11B, 17BG, 19TR, 19B, 19TL, 27C, 39C, 39R, 41T, 45BL, 45B, 45C(BG), 53T, 57C(BG), 59TC, 61CL, 61CR, 61B, 63BL, 63BR, 63C(BG), 64, 67R, 67T(BG), 71TL, 71B(BG), 71CR, 73TR, 73C(BG), 73BG, 73TL, 75B, 75TR, 77C, 89TR, 91C, 95L, 105B, 107BG, 110, 113C, 113TR, 113BG, 121T, 121B, 121C, 121BR, 121BL, 123B, 125C(BG), 133B, 139C, 141BR, 145B, 153B, 153C, 153BR.
Getty Images/Reg Lancaster/Stringer: 77B.
Koninklijke Bibliotheek: 31T.
Library of Congress, Washington DC: 2C, 9L, 19C, 21C, 25C, 27TL, 27TR, 29T, 39L, 45C, 45BG, 53C(BG), 59C, 67C(BG), 71C(BG), 73T, 93T(BG), 93BG, 93C, 103(BG), 105C, 105B(BG), 123C&BR, 125B.
Courtesy National Gallery of Art, Washington: 139C, 139B, 139BL&BR.
New York Public Library: 67TL.
Österreichische Nationalbibliothek: 17C.
Rijksmuseum: 2B, 17R, 25B.
San Diego Air and Space Museum Archive: 145T.
Shutterstock/Aerogondo2: 55C(BG); Africa Studio: 71B; Aleksandra Novakovic: 59TR(BG); Aleksei Gurko: 89C; Alexaldo: 151T; Alexyz3d: 21T; Ana Menendez: 101TR, 101TL; Anastasia Panfilova: 71T(BG); Andersphoto: 91T, 91C; Andrey Smirnov: 85B; Anthony Maragou: 71BR; Antoniya G. Kozhuharova: 91B; Artram: 121TL&TR; Atlaspix: 29C(BG); Augustino: 53BL; Bensliman Hassan: 57C; Bryan Solomon: 141R; Carsten Medom Madsen: 145B; Chianuri: 83C; Chiyacat: 145C; Christo Mitkov Christov: 113B; Claudio Divizia: 21T; Cristina Ciochina: 109C; CS Stock: 103C; Dragan Jovanovic: 139C(BG); Ekaterina Pokrovsky: 67TR; Elena Dijour: 83C, 107C(BG); Elena Ray: 127TL; Elzbieta Sekowska: 63TL, 83C; EniSine: 83BL; EQRoy: 57R, 109C; Etraveler: 77B; Everett – Art: 61BR, 71C, 105R; Everett Collection: 83TL, 85R, Everett Historical: 31C, 89TL, 123T; Fotobook: 115C; Francois Roux: 59TL; Frederic Legrand – Comeo: 31B; Hakki Arslan: 31BC; Haraldmuc: 91C; Hein Nouwens: 83TR; Huang Zheng: 31CL, 75CR, 75BL; Igor Kisselev: 27B; Inxti: 53BR; Isa Fernandez Fernandez: 59C; Jaime Pharr: 75TL; Jan Martin Will: 113L&R; Javarman: 103C; Jgade: 153BL; Joseph Sohm: 115C; Joymsk140: 75BR; Kartouchken: 31TC; Kavalenkava: 31CR; Kiev.Victor: 45TR, 95TL, 109R(BG), 121C(BG), 125B, 127C(BG), 127BR, 145C(BG); Kiselev Andrey Valerevich: 127TR; Kseniia Perminova: 109BR; Kuco: 83C; Kues: 115CR; Lagui: 83R; Lembi: 55C; Lifestyle Graphic: 31BG; Ligak: 139C; LiliGraphie: 83L, 85BL; Lou Oates: 89TL; Luchi_a: 75CR; Lynea: 63CR, 73C, 93L; Majeczka: 75T; Maksimilian: 145BG; Maros Markovic: 31C(BG); Marzolino: 57R, 61T, 61R, 101BL; Mathias Richter: 141T; Maxx-Studio: 121TL&TR; Meunierd: 55CR; Miceking: 141C(BG); Michal812: 19BR; Milkovasa: 83B; Morphart Creation: 7, 55B, 63C, 71B, 141BL; MrVayn: 31TR; Multitel: 73B(BG); Nagib: 89C(BG); Naypong: 145B(BG); Niall Dunne: 55TR; Nikonaft: 105L, 107C; Niradj: 107B; Nuruddean: 57BR; Oksana2010: 75CR; Oksanka0007: 89BG; Olga Besnard: 115TR, 115T; Onur Ersin: 85B; Pack-Shot: 71CR; Pakpoomkh: 55C; Paolo Airenti: 107TC; Paul Atkinson: 11C(BG); 133C(BG); Photomaster: 139T; Pigprox: 103C(BG); Pisaphotography: 31C; Prajak Poonyawatpornkul: 31BC; Premier Photo: 11C, 133C; Protasov AN: 85TL; Rainer Lesniewski: 77T(BG); Rost9: 77TL; Sergey Rybin: 53TR(BG); Sergii Rudiuk: 59TR; Sogno Lucido: 53TL; Spaxiax: 85B; Stefano Ember: 83BL, 83BR; Steve Collender: 57TR; Steven Bostock: 31BL; Svitlana Belinska: 105TL; Theeradech Sanin: 83B; Torsten Lorenz: 75C(BG); Tupungato: 41TR; Tusumaru: 113L&R(BG); Velirina: 141T; Veniamin Kraskov: 2BR, 25BR, 59BR; Viacheslav Lopatin: 101C; Vipman: 67BL; Vlue: 109L(BG); Williamxerez: 41B; Wjarek: 95TR; XC: 153TL; Yganko: 115B; Yuriy Boyko: 115L; Zvonimir Atletic: 103T, 103B.
Wellcome Library, London: 31BR.
Wikimedia Commons/Andrei Dan Suciu: 151C; CetusCetus: 151B; Citizen59: 141T(BG); Claude Villetaneuse: 11T, 133T; Clouet: 141L; Coldcreation: 141C; Copyleft: 61C; Geographicus: 71C(BG); Guilhem-Vellut: 113B(BG); Issael Falcon: 151BR; Jastrow: 125R; Jebulon: 131C, 131R, 131L; Khardan: 85TR; Marie-Lan Nguyen: 17BR; Mario Roberto Durán Ortiz: 141C; Moonik: 77L; Mu: 71TL, 89C; Myrabella: 93B; Remi Mathis: 109TR; Sanchezn: 31C; Shonagon: 131CR; Siren: 85B; Vassil: 131CL.

All reasonable efforts have been made to trace copyright holders and to obtain their permission for the use of copyright material. The publisher apologizes for any errors or omissions in the list above and will gratefully incorporate any corrections in future reprints if notified.